How to Soothe a Virgo

Real-life guidance on how to get along and be friends with the 6th sign of the Zodiac

How to Soothe a Virgo

Real-life guidance on
how to get along and be friends with
the 6th sign of the Zodiac

Mary English

Winchester, UK
Washington, USA

First published by Dodona Books, 2013
Dodona Books is an imprint of John Hunt Publishing Ltd., Laurel House, Station Approach,
Alresford, Hants, SO24 9JH, UK
office1@jhpbooks.net
www.johnhuntpublishing.com
www.dodona-books.com

For distributor details and how to order please visit the 'Ordering' section on our website.

Text copyright: Mary English 2013

ISBN: 978 1 78099 847 3

A CIP catalogue record for this book is available from the British Library.

Design: Stuart Davies

Printed and bound by CPI Group (UK) Ltd, Croydon, CR0 4YY

We operate a distinctive and ethical publishing philosophy in all
areas of our business, from our global network of authors to
production and worldwide distribution.

CONTENTS

Acknowledgements ix

Introduction 1

1. The Sign 11
2. How to Make a Chart 32
3. The Ascendant 37
4. The Moon 45
5. The Houses 53
6. The Problems 60
7. The Solutions 64
8. Soothing Tactics 71

Astrological Chart Information and Birth Data 90
Further Information 93
References 94

This book is dedicated to:
My book-lover brother Toby
and also to my lovely stepson Robert

Also by Mary L English

6 Easy Steps in Astrology
The Birth Charts of Indigo Children
How to Survive a Pisces (O-Books)
How to Bond with an Aquarius (O-Books)
How to Cheer up a Capricorn (O-Books)
How to Believe in a Sagittarius (O-Books)
How to Win the Trust of a Scorpio (O-Books)
How to Love a Libra (O-Books)

Acknowledgements

I would like to thank the following people:

My son for being the Libran that makes me always look on the other side.

My Taurus husband Jonathan for being the most wonderful man in my world.

Mabel, Jessica and Usha for their homeopathic help and understanding.

Laura and Mandy for their friendship.

Donna Cunningham for her help and advice.

Judy Hall for her inspiration.

Alois Treindl for being the Pisces that founded the wonderful Astro.com website.

Judy Ramsell Howard at the Bach Centre for her encouragement.

John my publisher for being the person that fought tooth and nail to get this book published and all the staff at O-Books including Stuart, Nick, Trevor, Kate, Catherine, Maria and Mary.

Also Cherry, Alam, Mary Shukle and Oksana, for their helpful read-throughs.

And last but not least my lovely clients for their valued contributions.

Introduction

This book that you are reading is part of a series of beginner Astrology books aimed at people who have an interest in Astrology and an interest in their Zodiac or Sun sign. It started with Pisces, my sign, and gradually grew into a rather large project to cover each sign.

As I'd started at the end of the Zodiac, I thought I'd go backwards and here I am at Virgo, the 6th sign.

The title changed quite a few times before I settled on the one you're reading. This was brought about by a combination of my Pisces wobbliness and the Virgo need for exactness and correctness. I apologise now if anything I've written isn't as you expected or wanted, but I've done my best to bring you a rounded view of Virgo.

Each book has been written with quotes from real people, people the same as you, living their lives on planet Earth. Full of questions about their lives, wondering and hoping that learning a little about their sign will bring some useful inner knowledge. Because, after all, learning something new is only helpful if it brings some sort of understanding.

Astrology is incredibly good at helping us to learn about our motivations, what makes us tick. Each sign of the Zodiac is different, and as there are only 12 signs, we could be accused of dividing humankind into rather small categories. However, as Astrology uses over 10 bits of information and 9 other celestial bodies other than the Sun that we take into account, by the end of this book you'll understand that the Sun sign isn't the whole picture.

I work in private practice in Bath, UK. I have a Diploma in Homeopathy and a Certificate in Counselling Skills. Quite modest qualifications. I am a self-taught astrologer and embarked on my astrological studies after my homeopath, while she was taking my case, said, 'That must have been during your Saturn Return.' As I had no idea what Saturn was, let alone a 'return', I went home and started studying. I read every Astrology book I could get my hands on. I badgered my uncle to give me my lovely deceased auntie's Astrology books and I spent endless hours making up as many charts as I could.

I already had a thriving practice seeing Homeopathy clients and also doing 'readings' for other clients. I read palms and cards – something I'd started as a teenager. I called myself a 'Psychic Consultant' and travelled across the UK attending private functions through an agency in Chippenham. I loved (and still love) my work.

After a few years of home study, I started combining the Astrology I'd learned in my practice. I must explain at this point that no one will spend money on a reading if they don't get the answers they need, or if they feel they've been ripped off. I take my work very seriously and can safely say that the majority of my clients have been happy with the service they receive.

Over the years I've been to various psychics and fortune-tellers and know the difference between a good one...and a bad one. A good reader will make sure that they address the current issues, offer some explanation for them, and will also offer sensible solutions to them. It's no good spending money on a reading if all you hear is, 'Things will get better.' Things generally do get better. The major question is *when* will they get better...and in *what way*?

Astrology is very good at answering those questions, as each planet that we use will move at a certain rate, thereby giving us a good idea of time scales.

In 2001 I was invited by Melissa Corkhill, the editor of *The Green Parent*, to write an Astrology column for her magazine as she'd read my article about Indigo children and had heard of my research. I happily wrote her Astrology column for six years; then, as the writing increased for this series of books, I sadly had to stop.

I now am a guest on the *Hannah Murray Show* on Talk Radio Europe, which has a listenership of over 1 million all around the Costa del Sol.

So, that's enough about me. Let's get stuck into some Astrology.

A Brief History of Astrology

Christopher McIntosh, a historian, tells us in his *The Astrologers and Their Creed* that Astrology was discovered in what is now called the Middle East – Iraq:

> It was the priests of the kingdom of Babylonia who made the discovery, which set the pattern for the development of astronomy and of the zodiacal system of astrology that we know today. For many generations they had been meticulously observing and recording the movements of the heavenly bodies. Finally they had, by careful calculation, discovered that there were, besides the Sun and the Moon, five other visible planets which moved in established courses through the sky. These were the planets that we now call Mercury, Venus, Mars, Jupiter and Saturn.
>
> The discovery which these priest-astronomers made was a remarkable one, considering how crude were the instruments with which they worked. They had no telescopes, nor any of the complicated apparatus which astronomers use today. But they did have one big advantage. The area, next to the Persian Gulf, on which their kingdom lay was blessed with extremely clear skies. In order to make full use of this advantage they built towers on flat areas of country and from these were able to scan the entire horizon.
>
> These priests lived highly secluded lives in monasteries usually adjacent to the towers. Every day they observed the movements of the heavenly spheres and noted down any

corresponding earthly phenomena from floods to rebellions. Very early on they had come to the conclusion that the laws which governed the movements of the stars and planets also governed events on Earth. The seasons changed with the movements of the Sun, therefore, they argued, the other heavenly bodies must surely exercise a similar influence...

In the beginning the stars and planets were regarded as being actual gods. Later, as religion became more sophisticated, the two ideas were separated and the belief developed that the god 'ruled' the corresponding planet.

Gradually, a highly complex system was built up in which each planet had a particular set of properties ascribed to it. This system was developed partly through the reports of the priests and partly through the natural characteristics of the planets.[1]

Astrology was therefore born out of careful observation and also a desire by the Sumerians to add meaning to their lives. At first it was for a practical purpose, to help their crops, then it developed into one that was spiritual, and thousands of years later, Astrology is still with us.

Definition of Astrology

Astrology is the study of the planets but not in the astronomical sense. Astrologers look at the planets and record where they are from the viewpoint of the Earth and divide the sky into 12 equal portions. Those portions start at the spring equinox of 0° Aries. We use astronomical information, but the difference between astronomy and astrology is that astrologers use this astronomical information for a different, more spiritual purpose.

Originally astronomers and astrologers were the same species, but as science progressed, astronomers broke away and focused only on the planets themselves, not on their meaning. They now religiously record all the material data they can get their hands on. The weight of the planets, the geography of them, the minerals and temperatures, the location in space, their speed, their orbits...on and on, more and more data is 'discovered'. However, less and less is learned about their purpose. Less and less about their reason for existence or their relationship with us here on planet Earth.

Astrologers believe that we are all connected: 'As above, so below.'

Just as we are all connected as beings from the same human race, astrologers believe we are all connected in some way to everything around us. Richard Tarnas writes about this at length in his wonderful book *Cosmos and Psyche*; he says that the 'new' world we now live in treats the solar system as 'objects' whereas he regards them (as do I) as something we are part of, not separate from.

As always, there is some synchronicity when writing a book. I have a Virgo brother who, while I was working on the book, visited our elderly mother (who I wrote about in my *How to Bond with an Aquarius*). She was in a chipper, chirpy mood and they decided to take a walk in the sunshine. It was a lovely sunny day and the ground was dry and easy underfoot. As they were walking out of the care home, Mum happened to remark (as she does when she's out and about – she *always* remarks on the things she sees): 'Oh, what a lot of stones! I've *never* seen anything like that before!'

The drive is made of pebble stones, and yes, there are a lot (when you think about it, but it's not something I think about); however, instead of my brother just letting the remark go, he just *had* to correct her (and tell me about the correction because we had a chat later in the day) and remind her gently that she had had a pebble drive at her previous address briefly when she first moved in. It was later tarmacked over.

My brother's point was: Mum *had seen* a pebble drive before...and that small imperfection, on an otherwise sunny and

5

beautiful day, *had* to be corrected...because it was just plain wrong.

This is something we will learn about a little more as we progress through this book. We will learn about the little things that 'make' a Virgo a Virgo. Their characteristics, their leanings, their likes and dislikes, and their motivations.

How the Zodiac Signs Are When They're Not Feeling Well

I have a confession to make. I have seen a lot of Virgos in my private practice and I have built up an image of them that may not be totally correct, and one of those centres on anxiety. Obviously you don't go and see a practitioner or therapist if you're feeling tip-top. That would be a strange waste of money! So the clients I see are all in some sort of anxious state. Don't get me wrong, but Virgos are more *obviously* anxious...and the difference with them is that they're more able to *describe* their anxieties. In reams.

I own pages and pages of notes of anxious Virgo people...and I sort of made the connection that *all* Virgos are anxious, which isn't entirely true...but when things 'go wrong', which happens to everyone, Virgos will lead the field in being able to *describe* their anxieties, being able to give every last detail of how they feel: what they had for breakfast, how long their last headache lasted and which side of the head felt worse, how their tummy is (Virgo rules the digestion) and what they ate that might have upset it...They make fantastic homeopathic clients because of this detail. We love detail in Homeopathy because our prescriptions are based on the exact symptoms you're suffering from, and we match them with something similar – not the same, but similar – enough to get the body back into homeostasis.

In a crisis an Aries will come out fighting, focused on the one outcome they want. If they're ill, they'll talk about fighting their illness, or tackling it, or beating it. They will turn up on time, or early; they won't want you to hold them back from 'getting better fast' and will want you to give them clear, sensible, do-able instructions.

A Taurus will go into a slump and want help with the 'now'. They're not interested in tomorrow, or next week; they want their symptoms to 'be gone' and you will have to work like a genie to remove their major symptom. If you don't manage to get rid of the worst symptom, like pain or sleeplessness, they'll be out of the door.

A Gemini will want to talk about everything, *except* what is truly bothering them. With persistent questioning you might get them to confess, but then you'll lose them because they think they've told you too much. It's best to talk about the weather and the funny-thing-they-saw-yesterday and keep the conversation flowing. They will start to improve just by being allowed to talk about 'stuff'...and eventually they'll get bored with wanting to get better, as they've improved, and you won't see them again.

A Cancer will want to weep and weep and weep as if they'll never stop the tears, and provided you've got a good, big box of tissues, things will be OK. Being gentle and listening carefully and asking them, 'How did that make you *feel*?' will help them and they'll soon start to improve. If they get better, they'll then send all their friends and family to you, and eventually you'll become part of their extended family, which is really sweet.

A Leo will want your undivided attention. They will text or email or phone to give you updates and will want you to congratulate them on their recovery and make them feel as if you do *genuinely* care about their recovery (which you do because an ill Leo is a really sad experience). They will feel better when you can help them feel surrounded by the love they so easily give to others. If you remind them of the fact that love goes round, and they are part of that sunny experience, they'll soon improve.

A Libra will mostly be concerned with relationships. Their partner, or lover, or close person. And how their unwellness will have affected that. They will be upset if they don't feel attractive to them any more and may accuse their partner of having changed or got fat, or not taking as much care and attention about their appearance. They will also be worrying about 'having to make a choice' about something, a terrible dilemma for a Libra. Too many instructions or choices won't work, so you'll have to be firm and suggest just one solution, just one remedy – enough to gently nudge them back to health.

A Scorpio will *not* tell you what's really wrong. Not now, not tomorrow, not the next day. They will tell you what's wrong with everyone else, and who's upsetting them, or getting in their way, or driving them mad. And if, after a few weeks of treatment, they feel they can trust you with their inner fears (which will be *so* scary you'll be on the edge of your seat listening), they'll blurt them out in a few long sentences and you'll sit there thinking, 'Wow! No wonder they're feeling so bad!' After this confession they'll come a few more times, and then they'll be better, but you'll be left with a residue of weird inner feelings which you'll have to exorcise with incense or white sage.

A Sagittarius has *all* the answers. They're not ill, and it's their mother, wife, husband, girlfriend, partner, brother, uncle or aunt that said they should come and see you. They know *exactly* what's wrong and they'll not take their tablets, and it's just when you think you'll never see them again, or they'll never get better, that the phone will ring and they'll want an appointment 'NOW' because they've decided their symptoms, which they haven't told you about just yet, are getting to them and they want them sorted *immediately*. As you've been watching all this unfold over the last few weeks, you know that just them admitting they're not well is part of the healing process, and they'll soon recover.

A Capricorn will prove a challenge to your healing abilities. They won't tell you how they feel because they'll be talking in negatives. They'll say, 'I *don't* have a problem with my digestion' which means they have, or 'I've *never* had a problem with my back' which also means they have. And you'll have to decipher everything backwards, and go back in time to somewhere a long, long time ago, possibly into a past life, or something to do with an ancestor (we call this *miasmatic* prescribing in Homeopathy = healing the ancestors)...and slowly, slowly they'll start to recover. They can't be rushed. You can't hurry a Murray...

An Aquarius will have some bizarre ideas. Whatever they're suffering from is something to do with something that they can't describe. It might have some weird name or come from some other dimension...and provided you allow them to feel free to visit as and when they feel unwell, and don't give them too many instructions or orders, and don't add to their already strange thinking by asking them to talk about their dreams (you'll be there all day if you do that!), an unusual, strange remedy will help them recover their strength to get better on their own.

A Pisces might – or might not – get better. There is no way of knowing. You will have to have strong boundaries in place or they'll phone you on Sundays or while you're on holiday. They'll be late for appointments, or forget completely, or get confused and think you're an acupuncturist when it clearly says on all your literature and on your website that you're a Homeopath. As long as you can help them sleep, they'll get better. They won't tell you they're better, and they might not even know they are, but if they start to arrive on time, and remember to take the tablets, and they remember your name, you know that they've got better.

Now Virgos are very good Homeopathy patients as they can give us in *great detail* all the symptoms we need to make a perfect prescription.

So, what I'm saying is this: not all Virgos are anxious, just the same as not all Capricorns are unhappy or all Pisces are wobbly messes (just most of them, not all!), but when they *are* anxious you will need nerves of steel to be able to help them, and this book will instruct you in how to do that easily.

And here lies the root of Virgo the sign: the desire for

perfection...which we will learn about in more detail in the following pages.

Mary English

Bath, 2012

Chapter One

The Sign

What 'is' a Virgo? Well, if you read the papers or magazines, the dates for Virgo are *generally* 24th August to 22nd September. I say 'generally' because it does depend on which publication you read and also where in the world and at what time you were born. This is because the orbit of the Earth around the Sun isn't exactly the same as our calendar.

In fact it takes 365.26 days for the Earth to go round the Sun. Our calendar is 365 days long, so every so often we have to have a leap year to straighten things out and sort out that .26 of a day!

In Astrology we don't have to worry about this because we work things out from the perspective of us looking up at the sky and seeing the Sun move round the Earth (which it doesn't do in reality).

If you were to imagine that we have divided the whole of the sky above us all around the Earth into 12 equal portions, one of those portions is called Virgo. We start the calculation from the spring solstice (in the sign of 0° Aries), a measurement relating to how the Earth spins on its axis. As it spins it moves from side to side, and as it moves nearer and further away from the Sun this creates the seasons of spring, summer, autumn and winter. By the time we get to August/September the Sun has reached the part of the sky that's the 6th division...and we call that Virgo. So a Virgo Sun sign just means that the Sun, that shiny ball of fire in the sky, is in the bit of the sky that we've called Virgo, and Virgo is shorthand for 151°–180° away from the bit of the sky we've called Aries.

Astrology uses astronomical data to make the calculations necessary to say what sign is happening at which month of the year, but as the orbits have nothing to do with our clock time on

Earth, the sign of Virgo changes at different times of day and night.

To make sure (because we are working with the analytical and precise sign of Virgo!) we have the right data, we are going to be using a Swiss website. More about that in Chapter Two.

Each sign of the Zodiac has a planet that looks after it. We call it its 'ruler', and the ruler for Virgo (and Gemini) is Mercury.

Mercury the Speedy Extreme Planet

Mercury's orbit around the Sun is four times as fast as the Earth's, so its year is only 88 Earth days long. However, it spins so slowly on its axis that one day on Mercury is equal to 59 days on Earth. It is also the smallest planet in our solar system and is not so easy to spot, the best times being early evening in the spring and early morning in the autumn in the northern hemisphere.

The American Space Agency NASA sent a probe called Messenger to explore the planet in 2004 and it became the first spacecraft to orbit the innermost planet on 18th March 2011. It was going to cease its investigations in March 2012 but has secured funding for an additional year of research.

So far, they have discovered that the surface of Mercury is covered in volcanic explosions, craters, and evidence of flood volcanism. The surface temperature is of two extremes. On the sunny side it reaches 430° C and on the dark side of the planet it goes into deep freeze with temperatures reaching a low -180° C. Hmm, don't fancy living there!

Mercury the Go-Between

If we look at Mercury in our solar system, we see that it stands between us and the Sun, and I agree with Christina Rose, who writes in her *Astrological Counselling*:

Mercury, positioned closest to the Sun, stands rather as one who introduces the solar energy to all the other planets, and vice-versa. Thus, his function is that of an introductory link, transmission, connection and we may liken Mercury to a go-between, an agent or courier between the Sun and the rest of the solar system. On an incoming wavelength, this function is experienced within the individual as recognition, perception and awareness. On an out-going wavelength, it is that which spurs us toward the communication of those perceptions and awareness.[2]

Astrologers therefore think of Mercury in the birth chart as something that acts as a mediator or negotiator and helps with communication.

Mercury the Messenger God

In myth, Mercury is named after the god that the Greeks called Hermes. And Hermes replaced the Babylonian god Nebo and then later the Romans named him Mercurius. Already this poor god has had a number of name changes.

In the Greek myths, soon after being born, Mercury set off in search of the cattle belonging to his brother Apollo. He made their 'hooves go backward, the front ones last and the back ones first' and hid them in the cave of the sun god Apollo.[3]

He is also known as the 'trickster god' because of all the naughty things he got up to.

Hermes was also the only god capable of travel to the deadly Hades underworld and back again. This is similar to the reality of the planet's surface temperatures being so extreme. Hot/cold. Mercury is depicted as a god with winged feet, travelling great distances at lightning speeds, being the messenger of the gods. It is these attributes that we mirror in Astrology. We're not saying that the attributes of Virgo are exactly the same as the planet Mercury, just that they're similar, that they have alike qualities. Mercury has a dark and light side: Virgo can be analytical and seemingly unfeeling on one hand, and attuned to health and healing on the other. It's these qualities and dichotomies we'll now discuss.

Virgo the Virgin

As the glyph representing Virgo is the maiden/virgin, we must not confuse Virgo qualities as being totally 'pure'. This is not virgin as in chastity but virgin as in not beholden to any man: 'Virginity is to a woman what honour is to a man, the symbol of the fact that she is not a slave.'[4]

So, Virgo is about thinking 'outside of the box', being free to think...and think they certainly do. If you want to tire yourself out, get a Virgo to record everything they think in 30 minutes. This is different from Aquarius thinking, which just goes into weird and wonderful places; the Virgo thought goes into great detail about the subject under consideration.

Here we have H.G. Wells, the science fiction author, who had Aquarius Ascendant (freedom loving) and Moon in Aquarius (also into emotional freedom), talking about his Virgo thinking in his *Experiment in Autobiography: Discoveries and Conclusions of a Very Ordinary Brain* in 1934:

I need freedom of mind. I want peace for work. I am distressed by immediate circumstances. My thoughts and work are encumbered by claims and vexations and I cannot see any hope of release from them; any hope of a period of serene and beneficent activity, before I am overtaken altogether by infirmity and death. I am in a phase of fatigue and of that discouragement which is a concomitant of fatigue, the petty things of to-morrow skirmish in my wakeful brain, and I find it difficult to assemble my forces to confront this problem which paralyses the proper use of myself.

I am putting even the pretence of other work aside in an attempt to deal with this situation. I am writing a report about it – to myself. I want to get these discontents clear because I have a feeling that as they become clear they will either cease from troubling me or become manageable and controllable...I write down my story and state my present problem, I repeat, to clear and relieve my mind.[5]

As he says, he's writing his autobiography for one reason alone: to clear his mind.

So what sort of minds do Virgos have and what goes on inside them?

Mother Teresa, a wonderfully humble Catholic person and charity worker, had a crisis of faith early in her religious career. She wrote about these failings in her journal which we can glimpse into:

Lord, my God, who am I that You should forsake me? The Child of your Love – and now become as the most hated one – the one – You have thrown away as unwanted – unloved. I call, I cling, I want – and there is no One to answer – no One on Whom I can cling – no, No One. – Alone...Where is my Faith – even deep down right in there is nothing, but emptiness & darkness – My God – how painful is this unknown pain – I have no Faith – I dare not utter the words & thoughts that crowd in my heart – & make me suffer untold agony.[6]

She thought that 'God' wasn't listening to her and that she was alone in the world. This caused her, as you can tell from this brief extract from her diary, an extreme amount of mental angst. She wasn't fighting demons; she was fighting her own thoughts, which were driving her to distraction.

As Eckhart Tolle quite rightly says, the only thing that is a problem in life is our thinking.

It's only by thinking that we 'make it so'.

In fact Shakespeare put it beautifully in *Hamlet*:

Hamlet: What have you, my good friends, deserv'd at the hands of Fortune, that she sends you to prison hither?

Guildenstern: Prison, my lord?

Hamlet: Denmark's a prison.

Rosencrantz: Then is the world one.

Hamlet: A goodly one, in which there are many confines, wards, and dungeons, Denmark being one o' th' worst.

Rosencrantz: We think not so, my lord.

Hamlet: Why then 'tis none to you; for there is nothing either good or bad, but thinking makes it so. To me it is a prison.

Hamlet thinks Denmark is a prison, but Rosencrantz doesn't…the only difference between the two views is their thinking.

But before we get too tangled up in Virgo thoughts and thinking, which we'll discuss in Chapters Six and Seven, let's find out a bit about Astrology and how useful it is to help us understand each other.

Characteristics of Virgo

So we have a ruling planet that speeds through the Zodiac and around the Sun with one side boiling and the other freezing; we have the god Mercury in myth, intent on getting his message across; and we have what astrologers call 'attributes' – things that have been handed down over the years as life qualities for Virgo the sign. She is also a female sign, as she would be, being a Virgin…

Let's see what Herbert Waite, writing in 1917, says are characteristics of Virgo:

This sign is of the element Earth, and of mutable quality. Virgo individuals are shrewd, discriminative, diplomatic, quietly active and reserved. They are often thought harsh and taciturn, but the fact is, they conceal behind a cold and matter-of-fact exterior the peculiar nervousness of their negative, mercurial temperament. They are extremely kind and sympathetic, yet so nervous and retiring that, many times, when expected to say a word in consolation, they refrain for fear the mention of the subject should revive sorrowful remembrances in their friends; in some cases their fear is that they may appear too sympathetic and not sufficiently worldly and businesslike. They, more than those born in any other sign, usually feel the need to bolster themselves up and even repress some of their finer instincts in order to keep their equilibrium. It may be said that they maintain their cool and dignified attitude and often impressive presence at the expense of an ill-deserved reputation for coldness of feeling; and thus their true nature is rarely, if ever, seen. When in authority over others they are rather too exacting, though just to a fault.[7]

Hmm, sounds rather harsh to me.

What about other astrologers' views? Let's ask Rae Orion in her *Astrology for Dummies*:

Nothing gets past you. You have an eye for detail, an inborn sense of efficiency, and a supreme sensitivity to the implication of language. You also have extraordinary analytical abilities, a rare clarity of mind, an enviable capacity for concentration, and on top of it all, an appealing modesty. You know you're not perfect – but you're doing everything you can to get there some day. As an earth sign, you are patient and industrious. Yet you're also an idealist and a perfectionist of the first order. You know how things ought to be, and you're certain that you can make them that way, one detail at a time. You're organised and disciplined – or you wish you were. And you push yourself to the limit. When other people try to wriggle out of unpleasant tasks, you step in, make a meticulous list of everything that must be done, and check off every item on the list. More work ends up on your desk than on anyone else's because, guess what? You're more competent than anyone else.[8]

Yes, that sounds a little more like the Virgos I know.

Let's ask the wonderful Linda Goodman in her *Love Signs* about her views on Virgo. They weren't (I'm afraid) top of her 'likes' list and she explains why.

She starts by describing a prayer she made (as a joke) to St Anthony, asking for her book to be widely read so that people would understand how to love one another through Astrology, both by recognising their own failings and by sympathising with the different, but equally ingrained, bad habits of others. She then goes on to ask for her book *not* to be banned by Virgos because Virgos make up more than one twelfth of the entire reading public, and as it was an Astrology book she also prayed that the Catholics wouldn't ban it, and the 'squeaky-clean' Mormons...

She continues:

The thing is, Tony, that I have no idea what the printer's Sun Sign will be. Of course, I could get lucky, and he'll be a Virgo. But just imagine if he should be an Aries! Could you maybe nudge him a little when he's setting the type if he seems to be about to miss a comma, or a period, or get the page numbers reversed, stuff like that? You just wouldn't believe the stacks of mail I get from Virgos, criticising a couple of author's mistakes and printer's typos in my first book, *Sun Signs*, and it's given me a complex. So I respectfully beseech you to guide both me and the printer of unknown Sun Sign origin in making these pages absolutely flawless.[9]

I agree with Linda on this point, which I didn't discover until I'd had my first book, *How to Survive a Pisces*, published, when a Virgo mom wrote this review on Amazon:

> '...*as a (Virgo) copy editor, I'm somewhat discouraged by the poor copy editing/proofreading that was done with the Kindle edition. I hope the print version is cleaner, because this one is difficult to read.*'

Reading and critiquing something is a lot easier than actually writing it. But in fairness we need both aspects in publishing, the providers and the editors.

How about asking another astrologer – a male one – about Virgos? Let's hear what Laurence Hillman has to say in his *Planets in Play*:

> Serving, organised, healthy, industrious, critical, pedantic, sensual, humane, sceptical, picky...Many Virgo traits can briefly be described as detailed-orientated, efficient, having discriminating taste, and being rational.[10]

Bit of a theme coming through.

Here's Marcia Starck writing in her *Healing with Astrology*:

> Virgos tend to be overly critical, seeking perfection in themselves and others, and are often too attached to purification and cleanliness. The positive qualities of Virgo manifest in service to others, a fine discriminating intellect, and a good grasp of earthy, practical needs.[11]

I think we can safely say that keywords to describe Virgo would be: orderly, analytical, perfectionist, health-aware...and anxious.

So for the sake of balance I asked a few real Virgos for their opinions.

Orderly

Victoria is an astrological author and writer. She lives in a quiet suburb of a large city with her husband and child. I asked her how orderly she is:

'Mentally, I'm very orderly. I hold a lot of plans in my head, mentally divided into different subjects, goals, areas of focus etc., and I spend a lot of time thinking methodically about how to do x, how to organise y and how to make sure z happens – and to be fair to myself, the things I organise mentally usually work out very well indeed.'

Grant is in his late fifties and lives and works in a rural location in South Somerset:

'I think I am fairly orderly as I have a place for most things.'

Janice is a mum and therapist and lives and works on a canal barge in the West Country:

'Very orderly. I always know where everything is at home/work.'

At the other end of the scale we have Deirdre, a lady in her forties who works as a healer and who is *very* orderly:

'Everything is filed/stored logically. (I'm self-employed and the office is the loft of the house so it's all somewhat combined.) I know where all my stuff is, but if I need something my husband also uses, I may have to search for it. It occasionally drives me nuts that after 15 years my husband still can't unload the dishwasher and put things back in the same place I've had them since we moved into this

house 8 years ago; places, I might add, that are almost identical to the previous house. (I don't say anything, just sigh to myself and replace whatever it is.) And yes, tidy is a must. The house may not be clean but it is always picked up. Including the cat toys (a never-ending chore).'

I love the bit about 'logically'; if that wasn't a Virgo talking, I don't know what was!

I don't do logic, haven't got time or energy for it...but then I'm a Pisces.

Analytical

My dictionary defines analysis as: 'detailed examination of elements or structure of substance' – so to be analytical, you'd have to break 'things' down into smaller parts and look closely at what you found. Virgos love doing this.

I worked with two Virgos who were dating each other. They were both drawn together because of their love of skateboarding. The company we worked for made 'toys for adults': skateboards, yo-yos, stomp-rockets, kites...you name it, they sold it. Everything was for recreation and competition. These two skate-boarding lovers, who loved each other deeply, eventually got a flat together.

I went to visit them in their new home and the conversation got round to tidiness.

'Mr Skateboarder is also a bit of a hoarder,' said Mrs Skateboarder.

'Oh yes?' I said. 'In what way?'

Mr Skateboarder went into the kitchen and opened a cupboard, and out fell a number of skateboards...and when I say 'a number', at least 5 dropped to the floor, but there were another 30+ of them crammed into this tiny cupboard. All the way to the ceiling!

Now, I don't know about you, but most skateboarders can

only skate on one board at a time. This lovely man had enough skateboards to last quite a few lifetimes...His devoted girlie was struggling with lack of space and clutter and yet here he was not able to get rid of the vast collection of 'stuff' he'd built up over the years. His first love was skating, but it had morphed into an obsession with *owning* the boards rather than *doing* what he actually enjoyed, which was the skating. To this day I don't know what happened, but I can remember my astonishment when he opened that cupboard door...

Here's Grant again talking about his hobbies and the details of them:

What are your hobbies?

'Birdwatching (main hobby), also model railways, steam railways, music (I play guitar, and melodeon [button accordian]), photography, reading (never without a book). I have a very enquiring mind and like to identify everything I see, from planes to butterflies.'

Do you collect anything?

'Bird data via birdwatching, musical instruments.'

How detailed can you be? Give me an example.

'I list the birds that I have seen in a notebook, and have been doing this for over 30 years.'

Now, to be able to list birds for over 30 years takes quite a lot of analytical-ness. I wondered while I was writing this section of the book whether or not there were many trainspotters, or as they prefer to be called 'train enthusiasts', who were Virgos, so I had a little search around the Internet and found a gentleman called Antonin Dvorak. (I found him by searching the train and rail-fans forums.)

Antonin was a talented musician and composer who also wrote articles on music. In his spare time he enjoyed collecting train information as this little (unconfirmed) report written by a fellow enthusiast illustrates:

Famous trainspotters of the past include composer Antonin

Dvorak (1841–1904). There is an interesting anecdote. A particularly interesting loco was due to arrive in Prague, but he had a concert engagement at the time. He was determined to know the number at the very least, so he told his future son-in-law to go down to the station and copy it down. Unfortunately, the young man copied down the number on the tender. Dvorak was not best pleased. He glowered at his daughter. 'So this is the kind of man you want to marry!' Fortunately, all was later forgiven and the wedding took place. It is said that a movement of the New World Symphony (not the one used for the Hovis ads!) was inspired by the noise of an American engine.

Dr Barry Worthington[12]

Perfectionism and 'Getting It Right'

Following on from the analytical theme, wanting to 'get it right' is one trait where Virgo excels. It comes from their glyph's image of the Virgin: of perfection, innocence, lacking intrusion and contamination. They will strive to get to that place of perfection.

Sam works as a solo musician and plays regularly:

'It is important to me to get things right. Hence I practise my music regularly. I get annoyed with myself if I get something wrong.'

I asked Noelle, a writer and astrologer, for her thoughts on 'getting it right':

How important is 'getting it right' for you? Give me some examples.

'I'm a firm believer in "good enough". Whatever I do, I do work hard at it and I do make every effort to do it to the best of my ability, but I don't stress out over whether it's perfect or not, and I will cheerfully walk away from something once I know I've done my best. Life's too short to obsess over the little things. When it comes

to what other people have done, however, I am quite critical. Even when I know someone else has done their best too, I will note things which could or should have been done better, although I would rarely tell them so.'

A little later on in our conversation she describes what happens if things aren't 'right':

'So long as I'm the one making decisions or calling the shots, I'm fine. When I have to rely on other people to get things right, or when I don't know what's going on and have to wait to find out, that's when my nerves and anxiety kick in.'

Chantelle is a holistic therapist working in a clinic on the outskirts of London, England. I asked her about getting it right:

'Getting it right is very important to me, as I am my own worst critic. "Everything in place and a place for everything" is an understatement! It is very important to me, because if a job's worth doing, it's worth doing right (first time).

'Other things are:
- *Good parenting (this is the most important to me)*
- *Being a good friend*
- *Generally being the best that I can be in the moment*
- *General cleanliness / good standards of hygiene throughout the home*
- *DIY jobs up to date*
- *Garden looking tidy, free of rubbish.'*

Note how she mentions quite a few other Virgo considerations: cleanliness, hygiene, tidiness (not that every Virgo is tidy – some can be terrible at keeping things neat – but they all enjoy having things in certain places), and I had to smile a little when I read 'free of rubbish'.

Here are a few examples of famous Virgos writing and talking about 'perfect'.

Van Morrison wrote two songs on the theme, one called 'Perfect Fit' and the other 'Perfect Moment'.

In Michael Jackson's song, 'You Rock My World', he wrote that he had finally found his perfect love.

In Leonard Cohen's 'Anthem', he sings about the 'perfect offering'.

Yao Ming is a retired basketball player and had this to say about a match he won against an opposing team before he came to play in the USA:

'If it had been Wang Zhizhi who had taken the last shot, then this game would have been even more perfect.'

I loved the way he said 'even more' perfect, as if there were levels of perfection!

Virgo Agatha Christie wrote a story called 'The Case of the Perfect Maid' in *Miss Marple's Final Cases*.

Virgos are so touched by the word 'perfect'. Here is an example from the author D.H. Lawrence, writing to his friend Lady Ottoline Morrell on 27th December 1915:

My dear Ottoline,
Your letter and parcel came this morning...Did you like the Ajanta frescoes: I *loved* them: the pure fulfilment – the pure simplicity – the complete, almost perfect relations between the men and the women – the most perfect things I have *ever* seen...They are the zenith of a very lovely civilisation, the crest of a very perfect wave of human development. I love

them beyond everything pictorial that I have ever seen – perfect perfect intimate relation between the men and women, so simple and complete, such a very perfection of passion, a fullness, a whole blossom.[13]

As you can tell from this little excerpt, Virgos love perfection.

Health-Aware

This is a subject that Virgos excel at. I can't tell you the amount of Virgos who are nurses, or therapists, or homeopaths, or physiotherapists, or chiropodists...anything with 'ist' on the end of it, and you'll find a Virgo. They like having an ideal to work towards, which is the 'healthy body', and will stop at nothing to achieve it. If you want to meet someone who's a vegan or vegetarian, look no further than our friends born in August or September; they will lead the field of health-loving individuals. In fact a gentleman called Donald Watson was a Virgo and he founded the Vegan Society. He was born on 2nd September 1910 at Mexborough in South Yorkshire and died aged 95 in 2005.

His father was a schoolteacher and he went on holiday every year to the farm his grandmother and uncle ran. He loved those holidays as his granny kept cows and pigs, but one day he witnessed the killing of one of those pigs and the memory stayed with him:

It wasn't long before the business of killing one of the pigs began. No attempt was made to keep me away from the scene; I just went there, full of interest, to see what all this was about. And I still have vivid recollections of the whole process from start to finish, including all the screams of course, which were only feet away from where this pig's companion still lived.[14]

He then explains what shocked him the most:

The thing that shocked me, along with the chief impact of the whole setup, was that my Uncle George, of whom I thought very highly, was part of the crew, and I suppose at that point I decided that farms, and uncles, had to be re-assessed. They weren't all they seemed to be, on the face of it, to a little, hitherto uninformed boy. And it followed that this idyllic scene was nothing more than Death Row. A Death Row where every creature's days were numbered by the point at which it was no longer of service to human beings.[14]

He became a vegetarian age 14:

It was a New Year Resolution in 1924. Did you ever hear anyone say there's no point in making New Year Resolutions because they're always broken? You can quote me as an exception to the rule, because, since 1924, I've never eaten any meat, or fish.[14]

He formed the Vegan Society in 1944 based on his conviction that 'they' were all wrong for killing animals to eat them or use their milk or body products to feed us. At the time he thought:

I seem to be taking on the world virtually single-handed, with no recognised qualifications other than a conviction that, with all the conceit I can muster, I am right, and they're all wrong! It's a dangerous state of mind, but one which, sooner or later, one can't dispel, and one has to go that way.[14]

He had quite strong opinions on health, brought about, obviously, by it being the main focus of his life, especially when it came to smoking:

I sometimes think now we're protecting children against the evils of paedophiles and it is still legal, unbelievably legal, for a pregnant woman to smoke, and inflict this poison on an unborn child, impairing it probably for life. I think, to use a religious expression, we must accept that the physical body is the 'temple of the spirit'. It mustn't be abused in any way. Everything we do must be to try to preserve it and feed it properly and give it everything that's necessary to prosper and live as long as possible so that, whatever the purpose of life is, we fulfil it to the best of our abilities.[14]

I hasten to add at this point that I am mostly vegan, and an ex-smoker, so I'm now biased towards his way of thinking.

I then asked some Virgos about their attitudes to their health.

Mandy is a retired schoolteacher in her late sixties and pays close attention to her health:

'I want to be a healthy person so I can stay active, alert and continue to enjoy my life. Being in my late sixties, my vision includes taking care of myself so I can have many more years of a happy life. Though I love well-prepared food, I watch my portions. I walk several times a week for about a mile. Also, I enjoy water walking and swimming which I do in a group setting as I live in an active-adult community where there are many clubs and activities. I'm involved in Nature Explorers, Metaphysical Club, German-American Club (through my husband) and I enjoy playing bridge. I love my friends, and enjoy a once-a-month luncheon outing with them. I am blessed by metaphysics and astrology. I use a few healing oils.

'For me, spiritual health is so important. When it's good, all other forms of health are better. I've always had a focus and dedication to some form of spirituality. Through astrology, I've learned enough about myself and others to understand that while we're all alike in many ways, we're also very different. This has brought me much self-acceptance and self-appreciation, as well as acceptance and appreciation of others. I've always had a good bit of tolerance and goodwill, but studying astrology has taken me to a *whole new level of understanding.'*

As you read, her attention is not only on her physical health, but her spiritual as well – and (obviously) I agree with her views on Astrology!

Chantelle's views are similar:

'My views on good health: I drink 1.5 litres of water daily, eat organic food as much as possible, take relevant vitamins and – other than that – everything else in moderation. Interests/hobbies and friends that feed the soul. My health is very good at the moment because I do what feeds my soul; I listen to my body (sacral) and not my mind. I have and do what I want, when I want!'

Sylvia is a mom to one child and lives in Toronto in Canada where she is a yoga instructor. She is very health-aware:

'Health is VERY central and important in my life. I work in healthcare. I am self-taught in many alternative therapies, herbs, homeopathy, etc. I have been interested in my own health since I can remember and in women's health since adolescence. Nutrition and healthy eating have always played a central theme. I became a vegetarian at 13 after reading Tim Robbins' Diet for a New America. *It was both an ethical and health-related decision for me. I have dappled in veganism and eaten macrobiotic, and followed the "Eat Right for Your Blood Type" diet for years.'*

Anxious

I was so anxious to get her home that after cutting the cord – I hate to say this – I snatched at her and just went home with all the placenta all over her…Got her in a towel and ran.

Michael Jackson on the birth of his daughter Paris

As I explained at the beginning of this book, I write about the aspects of a sign's weak points so that, by others understanding them, they cease to be such a problem for themselves or their nearest and dearest.

So what is anxiety and what makes it such a problem for a Virgo?

Anxiety is a state of being worried or concerned and can range from feeling a little wobbly because you've lost your glasses, to being out of your mind with apprehension because tomorrow you've got an exam that will determine your success or failure of the rest of your working life. And it's these levels that are so hard to quantify without getting tangled up in definitions and reasons and explanations.

I think we can safely say that being anxious, at whatever level, is not a nice feeling, and a Virgo will avoid it at all costs because, to a Virgo, their thinking is their most important attribute. If you disturb the way a Virgo thinks (remember Mercury being the planet of communication), then you're on a swift route to oblivion.

Here's Chantelle again talking about what makes her anxious:

'What makes me anxious:
- *Everything!*
- *Being overwhelmed with jobs to do – cleaning, laundry, sorting bills/paperwork*
- *Not getting enough sleep*
- *Lack of computer skills*
- *Sundays – getting the kids' clothes turned around for Monday morning: uniforms, shoes polished, homework etc., etc.*
- *Some days – just going out*
- *Commitments*
- *Socializing.'*

Noelle has thought about this a lot:

'If you'd asked me this when I was a child or young adult, I would

have said that meeting other people made me anxious, because I was painfully shy and probably suffered from social anxiety to an extent. However, that went away when I finally figured out that I could control my social interactions with others, that I could "choose" what kind of impression I made on others, and that I could choose to not give a damn whether they liked me or not; so I learnt that I was responsible for and in control of how I felt about social situations, rather than being subjected to what other people felt about me or about the situation. The whole choosing to be in control thing has been a big psychological issue for me.'

Sylvia again:

'Deadlines. Grades, tests/exams. Too many people when I'm not feeling social (e.g. a large concert with no seats, or a crowded space). Too many things going on at once (I can multitask, but it depends on what the tasks are as to whether I enjoy it or not!). Large cities at times. Money stresses, tax time!'

Daniella gets anxious when her routines change:

'Mostly, having my self-imposed schedule interrupted makes me anxious. I'm very much a creature of habit and when my routine is broken by something unforeseen, although I know I'll still get every-thing done, for some odd reason I get anxious about it. The few times I get sick and am unable to go into the office, I lie in bed sneezing (or whatever) and fretting. My mother has dementia and some other problems and I'm an only child – her health issues interrupt me and her changed attitude towards me (due to the dementia) makes for a not-calm-inside Daniella.'

As you can now appreciate, being anxious is not fun for a Virgo.

Chapter Two

How to Make a Chart

To make a birth chart (or 'natal chart' as they say in America) is much easier than it was when Astrology was invented. You don't have to look at tables of astronomical information or get out your telescope. All you have to do is find a good website and – *ping!* – all that information is free and instant.

The problem that most people find, once they've constructed their birth chart, is: 'What does it all mean?'

I can't tell you the amount of people that email me every day with a lovely, well-constructed birth chart. Most of them have found me through Indigo forums and ask me things like this:

Sender: *'Perhaps you could throw some light on the situation?'*
My thoughts: What 'situation'? Career, life, health, work, school, money? The fact that you've emailed me?

Or:

Sender: *'I've attached my birth chart to the email. I hope you'd take the time to look at it and respond to me.'*
My thoughts: Yes, it's a chart; what response would you like?

Or with even less helpful back-up information:

Sender: *'Am I an Indigo?'*
My thoughts: I get this one at least once a day. I don't answer these directly as it's not my job to make pronouncements just from a chart shape and there is lots of info on my site to help people decide. I don't want to be a guru!

Obviously, these are only my thoughts, not the replies that I send people. I quite understand that when someone has been struggling with something for a while, or worrying about something, their ability to be concise or descriptive goes out the window and I have to put my psychic hat on and work out what they *really* want to know.

No, making a chart is easy and anyone can do it. The trick is to learn something about yourself or your friend/partner/mother/teacher from that chart...so let's get stuck into chart making.

First of all, we need to find a good website that's free and accurate. Not an easy task as free-ness generally means it's been put together by someone who doesn't really understand what they're doing...or worse, they're trying to make money from advertising. Most 'free' information websites (apart from Wikipedia) are stuffed with adverts.

The website we're going to use is based in Switzerland in a place called Zollikon, overlooking the Zurich lake. The company makes its money from selling charts and there are very few adverts on there other than for their own products, which to my mind seems a fair enough situation.

Go to http://www.astro.com and make an account.

They will ask for your email and nothing else (unless you want to add it.)

You can create a chart as a 'guest user' or do what I recommend, which is create a 'free registered user profile'. This means every time you log in, the site will know it's you and it makes life much easier. Plus astro.com (called *Astrodienst* which means 'Astro Service') is a website that real, live astrologers use. It has over 6 million visitors per month and over 16,000 members, so you will be in good company.

After you have entered all your data:

- Date

- Time
- Location of birth

...we can now get your chart made.

Go to the page marked 'Free Horoscopes' and scroll down the page until you see the section marked 'Extended Chart Selection'.

Click on this link and you'll be taken to a page that's got lots of boxes but the main headings on the left are

- Birth Data
- Methods
- Options
- Image size
- Additional objects

Add all your info into the boxes if you haven't already, then click on the section marked 'House System' under the heading 'Options'.

Scroll down until you see 'Equal House' and click on that. This makes your chart into equal segments, and is the system this book is based on. If you don't do that because you're in a hurry or can't be bothered, then the information in Chapter Five will be wrong. The default system on this website is set to a system called Placidus, and so are most websites and computer programmes (except the ones I use!). This makes each house (which we will learn about in Chapter Five) unequal sizes...and to my mind looks scraggy and uneven.

Plus the Equal House system is the oldest system and the one the ancients used (before Mr Placidus came along and made some changes).

Now click the blue button 'Click here to show chart' and – *ping!* – your chart will appear in another window.

The houses are numbered 1–12 in an anti-clockwise order.

These are the shapes representing the signs, so find the one that matches yours. They are called 'glyphs'.

Aries ♈
Taurus ♉
Gemini ♊
Cancer ♋
Leo ♌
Virgo ♍
Libra ♎
Scorpio ♏
Sagittarius ♐
Capricorn ♑
Aquarius ♒
Pisces ♓
This is the symbol for the Sun ☉
This is the symbol for the Moon ☽

The Elements

To understand your Virgo fully, you must take into account which element their Ascendant and Moon are in.

Each sign of the Zodiac has been given an element that it operates under: Earth, Air, Fire, and Water. I like to think of them as operating at different 'speeds'.

The **Earth** signs are **Taurus**, and our friend **Virgo** and **Capricorn**. The Earth element is stable, grounded and concerned with practical matters. A Virgo with a lot of Earth in their chart works best at a very slow, steady speed. (I refer to these in the text as 'Earthy'.)

The **Air** signs are **Gemini**, **Libra** and **Aquarius** (who is the 'Water-carrier', *not* a Water sign). The Air element enjoys ideas, concepts and thoughts. It operates at a faster speed than Earth, not as fast as Fire but faster than Water and Earth. Imagine them as being medium speed.

The **Fire** signs are **Aries, Leo** and **Sagittarius**. The Fire element likes action, excitement and can be very impatient. Their speed is *very* fast. (I refer to these as 'Firey' i.e. Fire-sign.)

The **Water** signs are **Cancer**, **Scorpio** and **Pisces**. The Water element involves feelings, impressions, hunches and intuition. They operate faster than Earth but not as fast as Air. A sort of slow-medium speed.

Chapter Three

The Ascendant

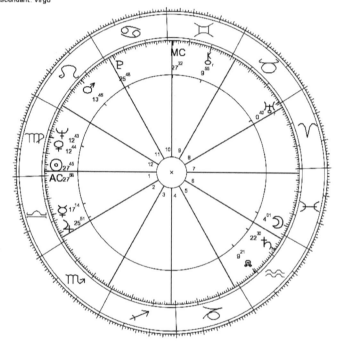

Name: ♂ Leonard Cohen
born on Fr., 21 September 1934
in Montréal, QU (CAN)
73w34, 45n31
Natal Chart (Method: Web Style / equal)
Sun sign: Virgo
Ascendant: Virgo

Time: 6:45 a.m.
Univ. Time: 10:45
Sid. Time: 5:49:13

ASTRO DIENST
www.astro.com

Type: 2.GW 0.0-1 18-Nov-2012

We are going to use the birth data of Leonard Cohen. His date of birth is 21st September 1934 and he was born at 6.45am in Montreal, Canada.

If you enter this data into the website (hopefully) your chart should look at little like this one above. There will be a number of lines going from planet to planet; they are called 'aspects', but we're not covering them in this analysis, so ignore them at the moment.

In this chapter I'm going to explain what an Ascendant is and how to find one out and what it means in astrological terms.

In Astrology the Ascendant or Rising sign is the part of personality that is most evident on first meeting. For instance, someone with a Leo Ascendant will be more bright, bubbly, in-your-face than someone with a Scorpio Ascendant, who is more likely to be someone a little secretive and retiring.

We determine the Ascendant using astronomy. At the time of your birth a section of the sky was 'rising' at that precise moment. If you were to look out at the eastern horizon at your exact time of birth, and you were an astronomer/astrologer, you would see that section of the sky rising above the horizon.

If you look closely, you'll see the initials 'AC' next to the horizontal line crossing the middle of the chart.

Now, I'd like you to imagine that in the chart above, the centre of the chart is the Earth spinning in space…and all the blobs in the picture are the planets in certain places on that day that Leonard was born. If you look you'll see the symbol for the Sun just above the initials 'AC' and the Moon bottom right in the sign of Pisces.

This is now an actual map of the planets' placements on the day Leonard was born.

The horizontal line crossing the chart is the horizon. All the planets above the horizon would have been visible at 6.45am. You wouldn't be able to see the Moon because it was below the Earth.

As Leonard was born early in the morning, the Sun was just rising; hence it is situated just by the horizon line.

Now, that horizon line is called the Ascendant. It's ascending or rising. And the sign it is in is Virgo. So we can safely say that Leonard was born with a Virgo Ascendant.

If he'd been born 2 hours later at 8.45am, the rising sign or Ascendant would be in the sign of Leo…everything moves every few minutes and changes sign every 2 hours because there are 12 signs of the Zodiac and 360 degrees in a circle.

Now that you have found out your Virgo's Ascendant, here are all the various Ascendants. Find the one that matches the chart you have made; the interpretations are below.

I have also included chart examples of real people so you can understand how each Ascendant slightly changes the Virgo flavour as it goes through the signs of the Zodiac.

Aries Ascendant

James Bond has a license to kill; rock stars have a license to be outrageous. Rock is about grabbing people's attention.
Gene Simmons

As the first sign of the Zodiac and one represented by the Ram, you can expect a Virgo with an Aries Ascendant to be more positive and proactive. As this is a Fire sign, the individual is more likely to react in a swift manner to outside events. They will be first in on the 'action' as and when it happens and will enjoy a good challenge.

Taurus Ascendant

What's so nice about Taurus rising is it says: I have the right to enjoy myself and if I want to lie on the floor and lecture, it's OK.
Zipporah Dobbyns

Everything to do with Taurus involves slowness and steadiness. There is no rush to get things done and, as an Earth sign, Taurus is more likely to be grounded and practical. There is a tendency to aim for luxury and satisfaction. They will appear solid and sorted and, as a fellow Earth sign to Virgo, will have the practicalities of life – money, work, home-to-live-in – organised and arranged.

Gemini Ascendant

Girls talk to each other like men talk to each other. But girls have an eye for detail.
Amy Winehouse

Of all the signs of the Zodiac most likely to want to chat, this is the sign. With Gemini rising, your Virgo will enjoy conversation of any shape, form or size. All methods of communication will be utilised, from Twitter, Facebook, to good old-fashioned pen and paper. If you were to have a Virgo with the Gemini Ascendant in your class, they are the one more likely to be doodling in the margin if they're not interested in the subject being taught.

Cancer Ascendant

My escape when I want to calm down is to buy some fabric and a pattern, and sew. And in the end you get something out of it; it's lovely.
Twiggy

Cancer is the sign of domesticity and home-based activities. It has the Moon as its ruling planet and consequently reflects the light from the Sun and enjoys emotional experiences. Can be quite sensitive. For a Virgo, this will make them interested in their family and home and less likely to want to travel the world and live far away from their roots.

Leo Ascendant

An artist carries on throughout his life a mysterious, uninterrupted conversation with his public.
Maurice Chevalier

No one enjoys showing off more than a Leo Ascendant. An appreciative audience and a long list of followers and fans help to keep this sign combination happy and fulfilled. They love an audience, love to be warm and giving, like to be the centre of attention. As these are all qualities so opposed to the Virgo traits, you might find someone who's a bit at odds with their appearances.

Virgo Ascendant

Curious things, habits. People themselves never knew they had them.
Agatha Christie

A Virgo with a Virgo Ascendant is a 'double' Virgo. So multiply those characteristics we have already discussed. The attention to detail and their ability to be analytical are magnified. They will write lists. They will tick things off their lists. They will write. They will compose. They will have an enormous capacity for remembering seemingly insignificant things. They will want to have their world categorised and put into some sort of 'order'...and if you've misplaced your glasses/keys/mobile, they'll know exactly where you put them. Photographic memory comes to mind.

Libra Ascendant

It's not just how they play. It's how they look, how they walk, how they sit.
Chrissie Hynde

Anyone with a Libra Ascendant needs to have a partner to feel complete. Until and unless that marriage or union has happened, they are likely to feel incomplete and alone. They feel best when there is someone to hold their hand, look into their eyes and reassure them that they're not by themselves. This is also the Ascendant that doesn't like conflict of any kind and will run a mile from arguments and discord. They love beauty in all its forms. They will enjoy being well-dressed and presentable. Their appearance is important and they might spend hours getting ready in the morning.

Scorpio Ascendant

Nothing that comes from the deep, passionate soul is bad, or can be bad.
D.H. Lawrence

The passion attributed to a Scorpio Ascendant stems from their ability to focus deeply. What that deepness is varies from person to person, but you can be assured that they come from a place of trust and want to cover every eventuality in human relationships. Famous for a heightened sense of sexuality. Hardly a boring Ascendant to have and more likely to reflect someone who enjoys feeling centred in the whirlpool of life. Capable of extreme amounts of concentration.

Sagittarius Ascendant

See how nature – trees, flowers, grass – grows in silence; see the stars, the moon and the sun, how they move in silence...We need silence to be able to touch souls.
Mother Teresa

This is not necessarily the Ascendant of religious belief, but of belief itself. Sagittarius is ruled by Jupiter the god of gods, and as such they view more than just the teeny things in life. They love travel, further education, learning and philosophy, and at the very least a Virgo with Sag Ascendant will enjoy foreign travel and long journeys.

Capricorn Ascendant

The two big advantages I had at birth were to have been born wise and to have been born in poverty.
Sophia Loren

Capricorn is the sign of hard knocks. They know them well. They're realistic, grounded and occasionally a little negative about life on Earth. They're matter of fact and to the point. Fluffy is not their game. Ruled by Saturn the god of serious thought, they will prefer a sensible approach. A Virgo with a Cappie Asc loves the wisdom of old age, enjoys serious pursuits and wants to be taken seriously about their ambitions and thought processes.

Aquarius Ascendant

I'm kind of kooky, but do I look like a religious nut?
Peggy Lipton

Crazy, weird and wonderful ideas are part of the Aquarius make-up. When it comes as a Virgo's Ascendant, its rebelliousness is slightly at odds with their Sun, and unless they can explain what it is they're doing, you as the observer will wonder what the heck they're up to. They love a true meeting of like minds and will be searching for zany connections that add spice and interest to their day. In fact, using the word 'interesting' will get their attention immediately!

Pisces Ascendant

You're in a different world then; you're safe because nobody knows what's really you or what you're making up. You're safe.
Julie Kavner (Marge Simpson actress)

This can be a more difficult Ascendant for a Virgo as it's their opposite sign, so you might find they say one thing and do something else. One thing is for sure: they are supremely sensitive emotionally and will feel sad about maltreatment of animals or young things. They will have a sixth sense that they keep firmly hidden away and will be involved in all those Pisces pointers such as dreams, fairies, angels and divination.

Chapter Four

The Moon

If the Sun in our charts represents our motivation and impulses and like the Sun in reality it warms us, then the Moon, which reflects the Sun's rays so it is visible to us on Earth, represents our inner emotional self. As we're not always so aware of how we feel until those feelings are acute, getting an understanding about our Moon helps us find our place in the world.

Some Moons get on better with Sun signs than others. An Aries Sun, full of courage and stamina, will feel a little lost with a cosy, sensitive Cancer Moon. So you'll find this person wants to start an exciting project and then their Cancer Moon goes: 'But I want to stay at home and bake bread, not run this company'...and this is where the difficulties start.

I'm not saying that we've all got multiple personalities; what I am saying is we're multifaceted human beings and we react in different ways to different things. The principle in Astrology is that the planets are archetypes inherent in our psyches. We've lived together in the same solar system for a long time!

In our chart example, Leonard has Moon in Pisces which makes him a bit of a softy, more interested in feelings and the esoteric than practical things. As his Moon and Sun are opposite each other, there is an inner dilemma about how he feels and what he wants to do. Being a singer helps, as he is expected to sing about feelings rather than what he had for breakfast!

The Dr Bach Flower Essences

In 1933 Dr Edward Bach, a Lovely Libra medical doctor and homeopath, published a little booklet called *The Twelve Healers and Other Remedies*. His theory was that if the emotional component a person was suffering from was removed, their 'illness' would also disappear. I tend to agree with this kind of thinking as most illnesses (except being hit by a bus) are preceded by an unhappy event or an emotional disruption that then sets into place the body getting out of sync. Removing the emotional issue and bringing a bit of stability into someone's life, when they are having a hard time, can improve their overall health so much that wellness resumes.

Knowing which Bach Flower Essence can help certain worries and upsetments gives you and your Virgo more control over your lives. I recommend the Essences a lot in my practice if I feel a certain part of a person's chart is under stress...and usually it's the Moon that needs help. The Essences describe the negative aspects of the character, which are focused on during treatment. This awareness helps reverse those trends, so when our emotional selves are nice and comfortable, we can then face each day with more strength.

I've quoted Dr Bach's actual words for each sign.

To use the Essences, take 2 drops from the stock bottle and put them into a glass of water and sip. I tend to recommend putting them into a small water bottle and sipping them throughout the day, at least 4 times, and to continue for at least a week, long enough for any emotions to subside and settle down again.

Remember to seek medical attention if symptoms don't get better and/or seek professional counselling.

Aries Moon

I'm not a sedentary person. I've always been active.
Lauren Bacall

As this is a Fire-sign Moon, you can expect someone who is active emotionally. They can get quite worked up about something, maybe cry or shout, then like a storm passing a little while later, they'll be fine. What makes them lose it is when they feel alone and ignored and not able to connect with others.

Bach Flower Essence Impatiens: *'Those who are quick in thought and action and who wish all things to be done without hesitation or delay.'*

Taurus Moon

It still strikes me as strange that anyone could have any moral objection to someone else's sexuality. It's like telling someone else how to clean their house.
River Phoenix

This Earth sign Moon involves feelings around physical, tangible things. How much wine or chocolate is left in the house, or their finances or their sex life. Things they can touch and hold, and feel their existence. They love velvet and silks and sensuality.

Bach Flower Essence Gentian: *'Those who are easily discouraged. They may be progressing well in the affairs of their daily life, but any small delay or hindrance to progress causes doubt and soon disheartens them.'*

Gemini Moon

I'm not trying to stump anybody...it's the beauty of the language that I'm interested in.
Buddy Holly

Gemini Moon loves language and to chat, and in talking about things they feel better. Writing helps, and their emotions are like the wind: changeable and inconstant. Emotionally they're aiming for understanding, so will read books and absorb tons of information to bolster their sense of self.

Bach Flower Essence Cerato: *'Those who have not sufficient confidence in themselves to make their own decisions.'*

Cancer Moon

I'm trying not to be alone so much and, man, it's a struggle. I want to get married. I want to have kids. That's at the top of the mountain. I've got to climb the mountain first. I'll do it. Just give me some time.

Keanu Reeves

The Moon rules Cancer, so feels 'at home' in this sign. However, it's a more family-orientated Moon than the Virgo Sun, so can feel a bit at odds for men (see above). They will be nostalgic, enjoying 'retro' belongings. The family is paramount and they will love cuddly animals and homeless pets. They will take parenting seriously, and mums will (generally) enjoy motherhood.

Bach Flower Essence Clematis: *'Living in the hopes of happier times, when their ideals may come true.'*

Leo Moon

An artist carries on throughout his life a mysterious, uninterrupted conversation with his public.

Maurice Chevalier

The Leo Moon loves emotional attention. To have someone paying attention to their every feeling is a super support for them. A bit of adoration goes down well too. They enjoy company, buying and receiving presents, and displays of affection. They love to shine and hate to be ignored.

Bach Flower Essence Vervain: *'Those with fixed principles and ideas, which they are confident are right.'*

Virgo Moon

I am not fickle. I am professional and precise. I expect the same from others.
Sean Connery

To have the Sun and Moon in Virgo makes for an individual who enjoys attention to detail, precision and preciseness. They will work hard at that which they enjoy and find it hard to relax if there is still one-more-thing-that-needs-doing. This supreme attention to detail can be a joy or a curse, depending on their job/occupation or life experience. They feel better when they're respected for taking the time to get things right.

Bach Flower Essence Centaury: *'Their good nature leads them to do more than their own share of work and they may neglect their own mission in life.'*

Libra Moon

Having achieved and accomplished love...man...has become himself; his tale is told.
D.H. Lawrence

Libra is the sign of relationships. Of union with another. Of marriage, partnerships and love, love, love. With a Moon sign for a Virgo, they might search for supreme, perfect love which only exists in their head. As Libra is also the sign of the scales, they will have to weigh things up carefully before they make a decision.

Bach Flower Essence Scleranthus: *'Those who suffer from being unable to decide between two things, first one seeming right then the other.'*

Scorpio Moon

I'm a jealous partner. You're entering serious bunny-boiler territory when Laurence even has to hold hands with a girl he's working with.
Billie Piper

Scorpio Moon feels in deep, dark shades of blood-red. They're quiet with how they feel but, like a burning volcano, eventually things spill over and all hell breaks loose.

Control doesn't always work, but the Virgo Sun will endeavour to keep those feelings on a tight leash. They are loyal and intense.

Bach Flower Essence Chicory: *'They are continually correcting what they consider wrong and enjoy doing so.'*

Sagittarius Moon

I think you can worship God in your own way. The important thing is that I know my Redeemer liveth.
Harry Secombe

Sagittarius Moon for a Virgo is all about belief, not necessarily in God or a Higher Purpose, but some belief in the wider expanses of the mind. A cultured mind appeals. They enjoy foreign countries and travel and feel better surfing extreme and/or remote holiday sites. The meaning of life is a constant quest.

This Essence comes under the heading 'Over-Sensitive to Influences and Ideas'.

Bach Flower Essence Agrimony: *'They hide their cares behind their humour and jesting and try to bear their trials with cheerfulness.'*

Capricorn Moon

Since I was 16, I've felt a black cloud hangs over me. Since then, I have taken pills for depression.
Amy Winehouse

On a good day, Capricorn Moon for a Virgo, ruled by stern Saturn, is responsible to family and those closest and accepts that life has ups and downs. On a bad day they're plunged into the heaviest of moods. They feel better when they know that what they are doing has some value to that family. They enjoy older company and being with people who have the experience that they'd like to become skilled at.

Bach Flower Essence Mimulus: *'Fear of worldly things, illness, pain, accident, poverty, of dark, of being alone, of misfortune. They secretly bear their dread and do not speak freely of it to others.'*

Aquarius Moon

We've been friends for almost 50 years now. It's kind of fun to be with her and travel with her.
Larry Hagman

For a Virgo to have an Aquarius Moon, you have to combine altruism, the planet, friendships and being free with their striving for purity. This Moon is more capable of analysing and thinking *about* how they feel, rather than actually *feeling* emotions. They also love technology and anything electric: solar panels, computers, digital devices; the more quirky, the better.

Bach Flower Essence Water Violet: *'For those who like to be alone, very independent, capable and self-reliant. They are aloof and go their own way.'*

Pisces Moon

On many an occasion when I am dancing, I have felt touched by something sacred.
Michael Jackson

As the last sign of the Zodiac and one that takes the rap for all the other signs' karma, Pisces Moon can be so emotionally fragile they occasionally implode with the stress of it all. They feel better playing with the fairies or dreaming, or looking after stray animals or those things that have been abandoned and lost. They can *feel* others' pain.

Bach Flower Essence Rock Rose: *'For cases where there even appears no hope or when the person is very frightened or terrified.'*

Chapter Five

The Houses

Depending on the time of day of birth, the location of the Sun in a chart can vary, so to understand this chapter it is necessary to have a relatively exact time of birth.

A Virgo born at 6am is more likely to have their Sun somewhere near the first house, as the Ascendant and the first house represent the Sun rising on the eastern horizon. This is where the Sun is as it just comes up.

So if you keep in mind that the placement of the Sun in the houses is representative of the time of day of birth, it will make it easier to understand what houses are all about.

If we are assuming that the placement of the planets at the time and date of birth is significant in some way, and our birth chart is a little map of the heavens as if we were looking up from the Earth, then obviously as the Earth rotates and orbits around the Sun the location of the Sun in the sky will alter during the day (and night).

Remember, Astrology is based on our view of the heavens. We use astronomical data, but we interpret it in a much more personalised way.

To make life easier, we are using maths and degrees rather than just vague concepts.

So there we are: we have divided the universe into 12 equal segments. Each one of those represents a sign of the Zodiac, and these segments are a fixed mathematical concept. A circle contains 360°. Each house is 30° in size. 30° times 12 equals 360°.

We know that the Sun moves in the sky depending on the time of day and night and also the time of year, because as it progresses (from our viewpoint on Earth) through the sky and sometimes in the year, it is lower or higher in its pathway.

You don't actually have to understand this to be able to get some sense from a chart, but it does help to have that little bit of background. All you really need to know for the purposes of this book is which house the Sun in Virgo will land in.

Just to give you a teeny example:

The Queen and the Astronaut

Queen Elizabeth I of England was born on 17th September 1533 at 2.45pm.

Edgar Dean Mitchell, astronaut (the sixth man on the moon), was born on 17th September 1930 at 4.30am.

Both of them were born on the same date, so if you follow the Sun sign Astrology you'd think they were the same. The Queen and an astronaut the same?

Not quite.

Queen Elizabeth had her Sun in the ninth house whilst Edgar has his Sun in the first house.

Queen Elizabeth had a Capricorn Ascendant and Moon in Taurus, whilst Edgar has Leo Ascendant and Moon in Cancer.

Their charts could not be more different, never mind all the other planets being in different signs!

Now that you have made your Virgo's birth chart, found out their Ascendant and also the sign of their Moon, you can now get some extra information by reading about the location and house placement of their Sun in their chart.

We call the location a 'house' (it used to be called a 'mansion') because it's as if the placement of the planet within the chart is like its little home. House = home. Which is just shorthand for saying something that might be far more wordy.

To be astronomically correct, I would have to say in Queen Elizabeth's case: 'Her Sun is located at 24° Virgo 3 minutes and 36 seconds, making her Sun located at approximately 108° at right angles to the Ascendant...' 'Sun in the ninth' sounds easier to me!

The First House: House of Personality

The secret of getting ahead is getting started.
Agatha Christie

As the first house of the horoscope is near to the Ascendant, having the Sun here indicates an individual who is proactive, self-assured and capable of action. This is not shrinking violet territory. They will enjoy action, aggression (not the violent sort) and energy. Good for project starting and leadership.

The Second House: House of Money, Material Possessions and Self-Worth

And some of the songs are about money! Let's just tell it like it is. If you turn on the box you get it... It's money, money, money, money, for several years now, non-stop.

The second house is similar to but not the same as Taurus and consequently displays an interest in that which can be physically experienced. As this is also the house of 'self-value', having the Sun here makes for a steady and dependable person who recognises the value of themselves and the worth of money and material possessions.

The Third House: House of Communication and Short Journeys

Boredom: the desire for desires.
Leo Tolstoy

The third house loves to communicate. Anything that allows this such as writing, phone calls, emails, letters, journals, or even just chatting to all and sundry, makes the Sun here happy. As short journeys are also connected with this house, you might find your

Virgo enjoys poodling along country roads and local highways and byways.

The Fourth House: House of Home, Family and Roots

I know I'm talented, but I wasn't put here to sing. I was put here to be a wife and a mum and look after my family.
Amy Winehouse

This is the house of home and roots. With the Virgo Sun here, matters are concentrated on nearest and dearest. Home education, home-working, being a housewife/husband or mother, or just cuddling soft toys and small animals, are important to this location.

The Fifth House: House of Creativity and Romance

Over the years I've learnt that you can discover yourself, your own style, through your instrument rather than through other people.
Kenney Jones

As the fifth house is associated with and related to the sign of Leo, we have a Virgo who may enjoy being in the limelight. Some form of creativity is necessary so you might find your Virgo enjoys making things, be it musical, artistic or dramatic. As this is also a Fire sign house, the Virgo Sun here wants to be active rather than passive, and if the red carpet can be laid out too…all is well.

The Sixth House: House of Work and Health

I always got my work done before playing.
Edwin Moses

This is what we call in Astrology the 'natural home' for the Sun sign Virgo as they are the 6th sign of the Zodiac. With the Sun here, all those Virgo qualities are somewhat magnified and increased. As this is also the house of work, this will be someone who can focus on tasks and be productive.

The Seventh House: House of Relationships and Marriage

Hold onto your man with your arms wide open – it's a great image and I've always lived by it.
Pauline Collins

When I meet a client with Sun in the seventh house I always make the astrological prescription of: 'Find yourself a partner!' This is such an important reality for seventh house individuals that without a partner they feel lost and only partially complete.

The Eighth House: House of Life Force in Birth, Sex, Death and After-Life

I liked Dallas *better because it was more deceptive; you could do more with it.*
Larry Hagman

No one is going to mess with the eighth house Sun. They have the capacity to endure and enjoy extreme versions of existence. Their intensity is matched by the eighth sign of Scorpio and can result in a Virgo who is tenacious and determined.

The Ninth House: House of Philosophy and Long-Distance Travel

There is one thing higher than royalty: and that is religion, which

causes us to leave the world, and seek God.
Queen Elizabeth I

The ninth house is concerned with higher matters. Those things that stretch our beliefs and philosophies. With the Virgo Sun here, you will find enjoyment in long-distance travel, further education and philosophy. At the very least there is a desire to travel and see the world. The longer the distance, the better.

The Tenth House: House of Social Identity and Career

I have contracts and obligations and business partners who are counting on me.
Claudia Schiffer

Now we have the placement of the Sun that is the highest it can be and generally the person was born roundabout lunchtime. As this is a high position literally in the birth chart, you will find someone who wants to get on and be successful in their career. They will also be concerned with how they are perceived by others and there will be a longing for respect and recognition.

The Eleventh House: House of Social Life and Friendships

I have no sense of patriotism, but I do have a sense of community.
Chrissie Hynde

This is a more sociable Sun placement and incorporates friendships and the social life we create with those around us with similar interests. The Sun here makes the individual happy to work in a group and less focused on intimate relationships. The gang, the club, the society, the organisation, the membership of a small, medium or large collection of people and interests resonates.

The Twelfth House: House of Spirituality

Astrology shook my belief in a rational universe and set me off on a learning curve which is still ongoing.
Marjorie Orr

This is a more tricky place for a Virgo to have their Sun sign as the twelfth house is similar to the sign of Pisces, their opposite sign. So instead of having someone focused, analytical and orderly, we might find a person who wants to blend into the background and dream their life away. There is a desire to touch the spiritual realms and play with angels or read the stars or even lie in the bath pondering life's journey.

Chapter Six

The Problems

You have learned a little about the Virgo personality; we will now cover the sort of difficulties you may come across. One thing is for sure: don't get down-hearted about those critical Virgo characteristics – they can also have a zany sense of humour.

Lenny Henry the comedian is a Virgo and I rather liked this little quote of his: 'I'd stay away from Ecstasy. This is a drug so strong it makes white people think they can dance.'

But, like every sign, there will be things that will drive you crazy, or things you just don't understand about your Virgo, so we'll cover a few of them here.

These are the sort of things I come across in my private practice and are based on real problems.

'My Virgo wants me to do things exactly the way they do'

This is a common complaint. If you imagine that your Virgo has spent millions of light years of energy thinking about, and working out the 'best' way to 'do' something, you'll then grasp a little about why they so want to carry on doing things that way. Now, this is different from a Leo way of doing things. They do things the same way because they've not really tried to do it a different way, or a Pisces who never really does things the same way 'cos they're barely on the planet...but your Virgo will have done. Not only will they have tried to 'do' whatever it is in lots of different ways to begin with, they will also have thought about it *so* much their poor little brains are now frazzled with the thinking and they just want the most peaceful experience. So there you are suggesting moving the sofa 3 feet to the left of where it was for the last few months/years in their home...and you've just basically told them that the time and energy they put into that placement not only is 'wrong' but also worthless. Don't do it!

You must also remember what sign you are. If you're a Gemini, you'll like to move things around here and there to give the impression that things have changed, because you like change...If you're a Libra, you will want things to 'look' a certain way...Your Virgo will have found, by careful deduction and experimentation, exactly how and why they like things that way, so save yourself the headache and leave things as they are. If something belongs exclusively to you, move it by all means, but not those things your Virgo likes a lot or owns themselves.

'My Virgo is so shy they don't want to come out and party with me'

This is generally a Fire or Air-sign complaint. These signs prefer and enjoy interaction with other like-minded people, enjoy the parrying of conversation, like 'doing' things and being active...and will wonder why, when your Virgo says they're happy doing book work or reading a magazine or putting something together, how they *can* be happy doing something so boring or uninteresting. I must make a case here for Virgos and boringness. Virgo is not a boring sign. It might seem that way to you if you're hurrying here or off over there...and there they are at home, stuck in some gripping novel or putting the finishing touches to something they've created...It's not boring for them to be contemplative. Not boring for them to just 'be'...they're very busy in their heads and that takes a lot of energy.

If you *really* want your Virgo to go to a party, you'll have to make sure there is somewhere they can escape to like the kitchen, or someone else there they really get on with, or the location or experience is something that interests them. Plus if you give them tons of notice (you won't have to drop hints, just give notice), they'll be more than happy to accompany you.

If you're first-time dating a Virgo, they might not be in a hurry to introduce you to 'the family' because whatever drew you together might not gel with the family's ideals. Unlike the Fire signs who will drag you to meet Mum and Dad almost on the first date, a Virgo will want to take their time and make sure they've briefed their parents first. Don't rush a Virgo. It's the quickest way to get them flustered.

'My Virgo doesn't seem to worry about the important things in life but gets upset if I move the cheese / leave spots of water in the sink / forget the name of...'

This is, I'm afraid, extreme Virgo territory. They seem to not be caring about what you're caring about. And I said 'seem'. They do in fact care a lot, but they just can't think about it for too long because the subject goes round and round in their heads and doesn't get resolved, so 'doing' something about the things they know about makes them feel a little better. It might not make you feel better, but that's where different signs deal with things differently. These 'important things' that you're worrying about will also worry your Virgo, but they know full well that they've already done as much as they can to alleviate the problems, and now in a truly Earth-sign practical manner, they're concentrating on the things they *can* change...which is where the cheese is located. And if you move their cheese, the world will end (figuratively not literally) because it doesn't *need* to be moved and if you move it, you're doing something against their mind-flow, which to a Virgo is a complete no-no.

Now don't get me wrong. Virgos don't like to think all the time where the cheese is located. They've already decided that on the second shelf in the fridge is best, because it's the mean temperature there and if it's on another shelf in the fridge it will more likely go off quicker, or get mouldy. They've already worked that one out.

Say they're going to make a cheese sandwich, they don't want to have to hunt for the cheese before they make it. They just want to make the sandwich easily, without having to think about the cheese or the bread or the filling...that's too much thinking. While they're making their sandwich they're thinking maybe about getting the car serviced, or how long it will take them to get to the end of whatever they're involved in, or they must remember to get some more ink/stationery/petrol/stamps/paint /coal/wood/crackers/moisturiser as supplies are running low, but I can guarantee that your average Virgo does *not* think about what they're doing while they're doing it...only if something is different or if it's moved...and you've now moved the cheese and all they can think about is: 'Why did she/he move the cheese?' 'What did I say/do/hint to make him/her put it on the bottom shelf, when they *know* that leaving it there makes it more suscep- tible to mould/deterioration?'...on and on...Small hint: Don't move things that they like or care about – it's not worth the angst.

Chapter Seven

The Solutions

Now that you have learned a little about Astrology, how to make a chart and discover the Moon's sign and the placement of your Virgo's Sun in their chart, you'll be on your way to understanding them better.

Won't you?

No?

Don't worry, as this is a practical book we'll also learn about how to make a few subtle changes in your life to ensure domestic bliss. Keep those Bach Flower Essences handy as you'll need a different one for each Asc or Moon.

So what sort of things do Virgos worry about? I don't have room in this book to list them all, but I'll show you a little example of a young lady who was struggling with her Sun sign's characteristics, her occupation...and her perfectionism:

'I HATE BEING A VIRGO
Traditional Virgo Traits:
Modest and shy
Meticulous and reliable
Practical and diligent
Intelligent and analytical
On the dark side...
Fussy and a worrier
Overcritical and harsh
Perfectionist and conservative

'The thing I hate most about being a Virgo is the perfectionist part. It makes me so frustrated. It's making me hate my own art. When I take a photo, I either hate it immediately or love it and start hating

it a week later. I keep on deleting more and more of my gallery just because I can't believe I could have ever considered those pieces art.

'The problem is that I've come to love art. I can spend hours studying artists and learning about different art styles. This has led me to want to be successful and wanting people to "adore" my pieces (just a little more feedback would be enough). Not just my friends, who like my art because they like me. I want to get into a good art college and make a living out of my photography in the long run. I want to live and breathe art and creativity...

'I know it sounds pretty desperate but when I'm taking photos it makes my heart pound and the corners of my mouth curl up.

'So it brings tears in my eyes when I feel so proud of a photo but no one else seems to share that opinion. It makes me feel so insecure and makes me want to smash my camera to bits. But instead I'll just write down my frustrations here. Maybe I'm being egocentric, wishing myself success. But it just frustrates me so much that apparently I lack the talent to live the life I want to lead.'

As we can see, this young lady wants to be a photographer but is so focused on being a *perfect* photographer that she hasn't allowed herself to just 'be' a photographer. And as we can also understand, she's cross with herself for even *thinking* she could be good one day. What a dilemma! She wants critical feedback of some sort and not from her friends. Luckily it got swiftly resolved when someone responded to her and put her work on an art website.

Remember what sign you are – that's quite a determining factor to your ability to get along well with your Virgo, and in this chapter I've divided the suggestions into the various Asc or Moon signs, taking into account that this advice is still aimed at Virgos.

Aries Asc or Moon

If your Virgo is upset, you're going to have to be quick here, because this sign combination moves fast. Here they will need some action. Aries is ruled by the planet Mars so the best solution for an upset Virgo with such a strong Asc is to get them out of the house for a *long* walk. Talking about this won't wash. The Aries Asc will want ACTION (as opposed to Leo who wants CAMERA! ACTION!). Tai-chi classes, judo, running, fencing, action-based sports. Not competitive as this combination is likely to bop you on the head if they don't get their way, and this book is written to help the Virgo friend...

Taurus Asc or Moon

Now the energies are slower. To make your Virgo feel better, get some cakes (low fat, sugar free) out of the cupboard. Listen for a few minutes, then get them booked in for a holistic, healing, gentle aromatherapy massage. Sooner rather than later. Taurus wants basic needs met and those needs are food, sex, and skin. The *body* is important here.

Gemini Asc or Moon

Get the kettle on. Get the books out. Quote the Bible (either version – they're both good). Have the books to hand. Discuss. Discuss some more. Look at workable solutions. Listen. Nod your head every now and then. Smile. Look confident and speak as if you know what they're thinking. Take them for a short, local drive in the car and they'll soon spill the beans. Get them talking, as the cerebral Air energies need to think and they can't think if they're upset, but talking about what's going on will focus their thinking.

Cancer Asc or Moon

Oodles of sympathy is needed here. Cancer is a Water sign and makes for a person who really needs *empathy*. You can't just cluck and look interested here. Unless you have suffered what Cancer has, you're out of the game. Best strategy is to (again) get the kettle on, turn off your mobile, look calm and sympathetic, lean into the Cancer's space, mirror body language, and get the tissues handy. Cancers need to cry and will generally feel much better afterwards.

Leo Asc or Moon

The second Fire sign of the Zodiac. You'd never guess it though because Leo thinks they are special and unique, and they need lots and lots of attention. 'There, there, there' works well. So does 'How can I help? What can I *do*?' The Fire signs like action; Aries likes physical action, while Leo likes company action. They want an audience to demonstrate and act out their story to. The more, the merrier! You won't want tissues; Leo has to be really suffering to cry and they tend to do so in the quiet and alone.

Virgo Asc or Moon

Now, I was tempted to say get the doctor round as Virgo is *so* concerned with their health. When upset though, a double Virgo will fret and fret and fret so you feel like screaming 'CALM DOWN!' This isn't a helpful strategy but does come to mind when you've heard *every* little detail of whatever was happening. A double Virgo won't really want to talk, as talking makes them feel worse. They will take a Flower Essence. Centaury is good or the homeopathic remedy Ignatia. Emotional upsetments will also affect a Virgo's physical health and they'll get tummy troubles or asthma or a whole host of seemingly unrelated health conditions, when what they really need to do is lie down in the quiet and turn their brains off for a while.

Libra Asc or Moon

Here you might need the tissues again. You will also need calm and tranquil, pleasant surroundings. Libra/Virgo is very sensitive to their environment and as Libra is 'ruled' by Venus they respond better to beauty and no discord. They might need gentle questioning; having tea is good, but far better would be a big bunch of roses or a gentle aromatherapy massage. Things need to be balanced for Libra/Virgo and fair. Everyone has to take a share of what is going on. Point out that if they consider everyone else's point of view, they will only tire themselves even more, so it would be best to find just one strategy to 'move forward' with.

Scorpio Asc or Moon

Not much is going to be visible with this combination. They feel things so deeply and intensely that if you were capable of seeing what they were feeling, you'd be a bit shocked. Dark colours, blood-red, deep yearnings. The solution is to allow them plenty of space. Yards of it. Somewhere where they can brood and ponder and yearn without it sucking everything into their orbit like a black hole. In fact if you imagine black holes you won't be far off what this combination is all about. If you're a strong person, stand within reach and be centred. If you're a bit fluffy, go shopping until they have recovered. There is not much you can do to 'help' as they will prefer to lose themselves in the emotion. They might write a song or a poem, get horribly drunk, or take large amounts of drugs. They might want revenge, so be watchful of this and aware that if there are other people involved when a Scorpio/Virgo is worked up, heads might roll. One useful tip is to get your Scorpio/Virgo to write a letter to the persons concerned, then ritualistically burn it. Doing radical things like this will help considerably.

Sagittarius Asc or Moon

If you can visit a church or spiritual retreat, or you know a Tibetan monk or two, it will help things considerably. The Sagittarius bit of the equation needs to understand the spiritual whys and wherefores. Like Gemini Moon, the Bible is good, but anything by a divine adept will make a Sagittarius/Virgo give some meaning to their circumstances. Oh, and they might make some very personal remarks – just ignore them!

Capricorn Asc or Moon

Be practical, realistic, and get the dry sense of humour dusted off. This combination responds well to 'old fashioned' good humour. Maybe slapstick, maybe old funnies. First off, get everything that has gone wrong into some sort of sensible perspective. Talk about the real things, the money, the plans, the future. Once they have a clear future-based goal, they cheer up enormously. You will have to discuss the truth and not hide behind niceties. Libra combis are happy for everyone to get on; Capricorn combis will prefer one solution, one winner, one loser. They'd (obviously) prefer not to be the loser, but generally in life, they don't expect much, so are rarely disappointed. They just expect everything to get worse. Try and guide them towards the idea that it is OK to have fun and enjoy life.

Aquarius Asc or Moon

Any major charity being mentioned will always help as Aquarius is the sign of autonomy and benefiting 'mankind'. I once recommended to a client who had a Moon in Aquarius in his life, to give money to her favourite charity, as that would help her understand how devoted he was to her. If you can bring the wider world into the equation, so much the better. Make sure their sense of freedom and individuality hasn't been removed and correct any signs that it may have, as otherwise you'll have a total breakdown on your hands.

Pisces Asc or Moon

This is the sign combination of sensitivity. Please be gentle with them. Imagine they are beings with gossamer wings, angels in disguise, beings from another planet, and you'll have more of an idea of how to help them. They won't really listen to what you tell them; they'll sense it, but you might feel that nothing sank in. It did. It will just take a while to filter through all the other 'stuff' that is in their heads. Light a candle, burn incense, lay out some Angel Cards or use some other form of divination to help you. The I Ching is good, and I know Virgos with this combi who will believe the 'oracle' more than the letter from the bank or the discussion with a trusted friend. So learn a little psychic technique or two and use them to assist you both.

Chapter Eight

Soothing Tactics

I try not to think about my life. I have no life. I need therapy.
Keanu Reeves

Now that we know the sort of things that a Virgo feels and thinks about, we're going to cover the various types of Virgos you're going to come across in real life and how to enjoy their company.

Your Virgo Child

Your Virgo child, like all children, needs to have some routine in their life. They feel better having something they can concentrate on and tend to like collecting things.

Here's my mother, Jean English, writing about my older Virgo brother when he was around 3 years old in her memoir 'Backward Glances':

He was very fond of jigsaws so we often bought a new one while we were out, so he could do it on the kitchen table when we came back from the shops. Sometimes he turned the jigsaws upside down and did them without the picture showing.

He also loved reading and books so much that when he grew up he became an antique book dealer.

What was more of a challenge for my mum was his eating habits:

He was extremely fussy about food and hardly liked anything. His favourite meal was crispy bacon rind and grated cheese…He loved strawberry jam and cream so we often had sponge cakes or iced buns filled with jam and cream.

I do remember him not liking peas or many vegetables and he once said nuts tasted like 'bits of bark', but since I've never eaten much tree-bark I can't confirm that association...

If your Virgo child is a picky eater, don't make a big fuss about it; just present the food as tastefully as possible and give them a few options about what they can choose. Helping children make choices always gives them a sense of their own worth. If they're kinaesthetic, food will have to *feel* right, so find out what textures they like. Some foods are crunchy, some are soft...you might never even think about these things when you're feeding a baby, but your Virgo child will have a preference. Virgo children are generally (and I say this carefully) quite easy to parent. They can be quite happy stuck into a game and not need tons of instruction. They might be more shy than other signs, but do keep in mind their Ascendant and Moon sign, as these will help you differentiate what's needed and when. The Moon comes into play when emotions are involved, and the Ascendant, which was determined by their time of birth, will guide you when they start a project, begin something or go somewhere for the first time. A Virgo child with a Leo Ascendant, for instance, will start things quickly, be a bit impatient (all the Fire signs are), be less stage-struck and more capable of appearing sun-like and friendly.

Here's a mom talking about her Virgo daughter:

'Picky eater – she'd rather go to bed hungry than eat certain foods. Every time she hears about an illness she wants me to take her to the doctor for a check-up. She takes her own bedding when she goes away overnight. This weekend we went away and she burst into tears because her room was not up to her standards.'

To understand your Virgo child and prevent too many tears and upsetments, keep in mind that they want, as astrologer Maritha Pottenger says: 'to shine for their competence, for being pragmatic and for their discretion...In an ironic twist you are likely to seek notice for your ability to avoid notice!'[15]

My stepson is a carpenter. And a jolly good one at that. So good in fact that at age 19 he won 'Best Carpenter in the West Country'. The reason I mention this is that his attention to detail has helped him in his career choice, rather than hindered. He hasn't bragged about this award and he didn't submit the entry; his employers did as they could see how good he was at his work. So if you're thinking about what job your Virgo child might be good at when they grow up, something where they can use those questioning, detailed faculties will help.

Your Virgo Boss

If your employer is a Virgo, please remember all the advice I've given already. Don't move or change things they like, be quiet and gentle, don't do sudden unexpected things too often, and they'll be friends for life if you know where the First Aid box and the painkillers are. I've never had a Virgo boss myself that I'm aware of, as most of the Virgos I know are self-employed.

I agree with Linda Goodman who says: 'The Typical Virgo is at his best as the power behind the throne, the one who dependably carries through the original ideas of others.'

The point she is making here is that a Virgo feels better being the support of an organisation, rather than the steering force. They're happier in the background, making sure everything is done in the right way and systems have been implemented correctly.

I know a number of Virgo nurses, and they take their jobs very seriously. I often say I'd rather have an injection from a Virgo nurse than any other sign. At the very least, they'll make sure I get the correct amount of medication!

If your boss is a Virgo and you can pay attention to what he/she pays attention to, you'll have a smoother ride.

Here's Janette talking about her Virgo boss at the PR agency where they worked:

'Highly successful, and ruthless, in business, his second wife was also highly successful in business, both of them at an international level, and he valued that and appeared to have no objections or jealousies about that. Rather, I think it was almost a need. Was highly critical of others, but was probably less so in later years. Used to exaggerate wildly, and was comfortable with PR style, a field we worked in for a while. Money was exceedingly important as a mark of his success and, I think, he genuinely believed he had no money, moaned about being hard up and yet, almost in the same breath, boasted about his shares etc.'

This is obviously an older man and a male perspective. Not all Virgo bosses are 'ruthless with money' – I think that's more the business territory – but notice how she described him as 'highly critical of others'...there's that Virgo need for perfection at work there!

Astrological Love Tips

I have written in my other books that to learn how to date a sign successfully, you must understand at the very least someone's Sun sign, so you can be prepared for any little quirks of nature. And I must also re-emphasise that you must also keep in mind what sign you are and how those two energies are going to go together.

If you're an Earth sign, you're more likely to get on better with other Earth signs and the Water signs...and so on. The elements need to match something in your chart. Maybe your Ascendant is the same element as your intended's, which certainly helps mutual understanding. But I must add one important proviso.

No matter how compatible someone's chart might be with yours, only real-life connection can make that on-paper relationship authentic. A long time ago I had a client who was convinced that because her chart was so compatible with Michael Jackson's she'd end up dating and marrying him. What she'd completely missed was the fact that she lived in another country, wasn't prepared to travel to the USA, didn't have a job that would even bring her into his social circle...the list went on. And even if, on paper, this so-called potential relationship looks like a match made in heaven, if you aren't prepared to put in some effort to make it work, you'll be disappointed.

That said, let's learn a little about the dating process:

Your Virgo (Female) Lover

If you want to successfully date a Virgo lady, you will need to understand what they're looking for, and what better place to find that than on a dating site.

Here we have a UK-based lady looking for her Mr Right:

'I'm looking for someone really special, for a long-term relationship in the future, but also looking for like-minded friends. Or perhaps I have enough of them really as I'm quite busy trying to finish my MSc in Environmental Conservation Management, get a job etc.

'I'm nearly vegetarian and sometimes even vegan but I don't rule out fish! In the long term I'd like to move either to a smaller town or perhaps back to the city, though I think I've had enough of city life really. It's too noisy / too much traffic and I also love getting out "into nature" as it were. I love music and dance sometimes as well. Also do a bit of yoga. Read poetry occasionally and more often the I (or The Guardian for a treat). Love falling asleep on train journeys...I love to travel in fact, and would love to go back to Nepal or perhaps go to India, next winter? If I could find a travelling companion it would be even better! Also love the Greek islands although I have to cover up in the sun now as my skin suffers. The Lake District, Ireland and Scotland are some more places that I'd love to explore some more. I wouldn't mind camping even and love real fires.

'I guess I'll have to go where the (paid) work is in the end. Well, if you think we've got something in common, get in touch! I don't

have a car so I'm limited to public transport, or lifts (or cycling in good weather…). I'm not really into sport of any description (or the Olympics for that matter), but of course we don't have to share EVERY interest!

'I love mountains – did I say that? As well as outdoor swimming, weather permitting! Also important, someone to live with or near, in the long term i.e. cuddles / keep each other warm and sunny in the winter! I love cats, but not so keen on dogs, although that could change, I guess…Although I'm a Virgo (I try not to believe in it, as a scientist, of sorts!), I also have a very strong Libran Ascendant and my Moon is in Sagittarius, so there!'

We have to read between the lines here to find out what she really wants. And I loved the way she was 'nearly' vegetarian. One thing for sure, you can tell she's being perfectly honest. There is no attempt to conceal here.

She also wants to get a qualification. Virgos love learning (that's the Mercury influence) so, to date her successfully, you'll have to not mind her with her head in a book, or going to classes or studying. What you can tell from this little excerpt is that she's looking for someone who will take the reins. Unlike an Aquarius or Sagittarius, she's not looking for freedom. Unlike a Cancer, Leo or Scorpio, she's not looking for 100% devotion.

She doesn't mind where she lives, as long as it's 'near' to the person she's dating. Notice she doesn't mention wanting to 'wash his socks' or 'make his dinner'. This is not someone who's going to be too happy with cosy domesticity. And notice also how she's gentle in her approach. She's a bit uncertain about what she actually wants and she's also not asking for dramatic displays of affection. Notice also that she doesn't like sport. Pay attention to that if you're sporty yourself. Unless your Virgo has got Aries planets, sport won't be top of the list.

Knowledge, gentle exercise, quiet surroundings…these will all fit the bill nicely. She hasn't described what she's looking for as most people on dating sites describe themselves rather than their desires, but you can get a feel of the sort of person she is.

Your Virgo (Male) Lover

Remember that Virgo is ruled by Mercury, the planet of communication, so top of your Virgo man's 'wanted' list won't be love. Unlike a Libra or a Leo that wants undying love-and-attention, your Virgo man will want some sort of shared interest that you will be able to work at, or talk about or do together.

My grandfather was a Virgo and his wife (my granny) was a Gemini. They met while at an art class in Portsmouth and married in 1915. Grandpa painted in oils and Grandma liked water-colour, but it was that first interest that drew them together. To successfully date a Virgo man you'll have to either have a joint interest or, at the very least, not mind them having their interest.

They're not generally so interested in nightclubbing and raving 24/7.

Here's a Virgo gentleman on a dating site describing himself (again he hasn't described what he's looking for!):

'Thoughtful and intelligent. Habitually not very articulate, and too independent, but learning! An ex-London ex-Edinburgh ex-Findhorn Quaker seeker. A critical/analytical Virgo; very particular. In an open-minded way. Trying to be careful, sensitive, respectful and kind to everyone. If they deserve it. Or even if they don't seem to. But I fade out from uncongenial situations, conversations.

'Feeling the need to surround ourselves with beautiful things...everything we have and use should be efficient, economical to produce from natural materials, and looking good but not pretentious. Comfortable to live with (i.e. not modern cars).

'All of which is a significant part of making the world a better place.

'My work is designing beautiful wooden boats, and helping folk

to build them. They find it a useful experience in careful skilled creative work, and very satisfying. And good fun. The designs are a clever blend of traditional styles with more modern methods and performance.

'Also busy with traditional music, storytelling, writing, reading, mediaeval calligraphy, photographing, model-making.

'I am fascinated with the West Coast, and the Isle of Skye; the cultural, musical traditions and folklore of the outer edge of Europe. And the Celtic way of being.'

Oh, I *so* loved how he wrote about how things he has are 'efficient'. That's a Virgo keyword. Notice also how he writes more about what he *does* than the whole dating thing, as if that's actually more important to him than having a partner. He knows what he likes and she will have to like that too!

What to Do if Your Virgo Relationship Ends

Ending a relationship, or being in one that ends, is always a painful process. There are no simple solutions, and time is the only thing that will help heal the hurt. However, with a little knowledge of Astrology you can make the process less stressful and more empowering.

If your Virgo relationship has ended, it will take a bit of time to untangle yourself from the 'he said this, she said that' that comes with the Mercury-ruled sign's attitude.

Fire sign

If you are a Fire sign – Aries, Leo or Sagittarius – you will need something active and exciting to help you get over your relationship ending.

You will also need to use the element of Fire in your healing process.

Get a nice night-light candle, light it and recite: 'I ... (your name) do let you ... (your ex-Virgo's name) go, in freedom and with love, so that I am free to attract my true soul-love.'

Leave the night light in a safe place to completely burn away. Allow at least an hour. In the meantime gather up any belongings or possessions that are your now ex-lover's and deliver them back to your Virgo. It's polite to telephone first and notify your ex when you will be arriving.

If you have any photos of you together or other mementos or even gifts, don't be in a rush to destroy them, as some Fire signs are prone to do. Better to put them away in a box in the attic or garage until you feel a little less upset.

In a few months' time, go through the box and keep the things you like and give away the things you don't.

Earth sign

If you are an Earth sign – Taurus, Virgo or Capricorn – you will feel less inclined to do something dramatic or outrageous. It might also take you slightly longer to recover your equilibrium, so allow yourself a few weeks and a maximum of three months to grieve.

You will be using the Earth element to help your healing, with the use of some trusty crystals.

The best crystals to use are the ones associated with your Sun sign and also with protection.

Taurus = Emerald

Virgo = Agate

Capricorn = Onyx

Cleanse your crystal in fresh running water. Wrap it in some pretty silk fabric, then go on a walk into the countryside. When you find a suitable spot that is quiet and where you won't be disturbed, dig a small hole and place your crystal in the ground.

Spend a few minutes thinking about your relationship, the good times and the bad. Forgive yourself for any mistakes you may have made.

Imagine a beautiful plant growing from the ground where

you have buried your crystal, and the plant blossoming and growing strong.

This will represent your new love that will be with you when the time is right.

Air sign

If you're an Air sign – Gemini, Libra or Aquarius – you might want to talk about what happened first, before you finish the relationship. Air signs need reasons and answers, and can waste precious life-energy looking for those answers. You might need to meet with your Virgo to tell him/her exactly what you think/thought about his/her opinions, ideas and thoughts. You might also be tempted to tell him/her what you think about them now, which I do *not* recommend.

Far better to put those thoughts into a tangible form by writing a letter to your ex-Virgo. It is not a letter that you are actually going to post, but you are going to put into it as much energy *as if* you were actually going to send it.

Write to them thus: 'Dear Virgo, I hope you will be happy now in your new life, but there are a few things I would like to know and understand before I say goodbye.'

Then list all the annoying, aggravating, upsetting ideas that your (now ex) Virgo indulged in. Make a list as long as you like. Put in as much detail as you feel comfortable with, including things like how many times they told you off for doing something, or wouldn't meet your friends, or fussed over this and that.

Keep writing till you can write no more, then end your letter with something like: 'Even though we were not suited, and I suffered because of this, I wish you well on your path.' Or some other positive comment.

Then tear your letter into teeny little pieces and put them into a small container. We are now going to use the element of Air to rectify the situation.

Take a trip to somewhere windy and high, like the top of a hill, and when you're ready, open your container and sprinkle a few random pieces of your letter into the wind. Don't use the entire letter or you run the risk of littering, just enough pieces to be significant. Watch those little pieces of paper fly into the distance and imagine them connecting with the nature spirits.

Put the remaining pieces of paper in the rubbish. Your relationship has now ended.

Water sign

If you are a Water sign – Cancer, Scorpio or Pisces – you might find it more difficult to recover quickly from your relationship. You might find yourself weeping at inopportune moments, or when you hear your song on the radio, or when you see other couples happily being in each other's company. You might lie awake at night worrying that you have ruined your life, and your ex-Virgo is having all the fun. As you might have gathered by now, this is unlikely. Your ex might be as upset as you.

Your emotional healing therefore needs to incorporate the Water element.

As you are capable of weeping for England, the next time you are in floods of tears capture one small teardrop and place it into a small glass. Have one handy just for this purpose. Decorate it if you feel like it. Small flowers, stars, or twinkly things.

Now fill your glass to the top with tap water and place it on a table.

Then recite the following:

'This loving relationship with you … (your ex-Virgo's name) has ended.
I reach out across time and space to you.
My tears will wash away the hurt I feel.
I release you from my heart, mind and soul.
We part in peace.'

And then slowly drink the water. Imagine your hurt dissolving away, freeing you from all anxieties and releasing you from sadness.

Then spend the next few weeks being nice to yourself. If you need to talk, find someone you trust, and confide in them. Keep the tissues handy.

Your Virgo Friend

Virgo friendship can manifest in lots of different ways, but you're more likely to find it's associated with your place of work or the club or organisation you belong to or the hobby you may have. You're less likely to be friends with a Virgo if you don't have some joint interest. As I mentioned earlier, the Virgo people I know have been met through my work in the therapy/healing sector. They're more attracted to health and healing as Virgo governs these subjects.

To get the best from your Virgo friendship, you don't need to see them all the time. It's mostly the Fire signs that need constant attention and communication. My older Aquarius sister has a Virgo friend she's known for years. They dated a long while back, but they still meet up for a country walk-and-talk and they're both very happy with the arrangement. Aquarians love friendship (more than love – see my book *How to Bond with an Aquarius* for more info) and Virgos like someone to discuss and debate and think about and muse and communicate with.

If you think about Mercury's speedy orbit, going faster than the Earth, and then three or four times a year going retrograde, it almost describes how a Virgo friendship will manifest in real life. Some weeks you'll see them a lot and things will be interesting and invigorating; other weeks there will be a lull while something else happens in their life. They're not being rude when they don't contact you; they're just absorbed in something else.

If you've ever followed Stephen Fry on Twitter, you'll notice that some days he does nothing but tweet, hundreds of them...then there is a lull as he gets involved in whatever he's doing...then he's back tweeting again. He has Moon in Leo but I don't have a birth time (trust me, I've asked enough times) and can't say what his Ascendant is...but if you want to get an idea of how a Virgo thinks, check him out. It's quite exhausting for a Pisces!

Incidentally if you're a Water sign and overly emotional, this can tire a Virgo. Here's a Pisces lady talking about a practical Virgo friend of hers:

> *'In the mid 1980s I was blessed with a Virgo friend who banged on the table one time and told me to stop expecting everyone else to make my decisions for me.'*

Your Virgo friend won't generally abandon you when times are tough and will expect reciprocal treatment if they fall on hard times. They might also spot if you're sliding into depression or anxiety and offer practical help like remedies or contact details for therapists they've used.

Your Virgo Mother

I have met many a Virgo mum, as I am a mum myself, but the one I'm just about to tell you about I have never met.

A very nice Pisces gentleman that I know has a Virgo mother called Jacqueline. He is remarried but has been with his new wife, Shirley, for over 30 years. Every Christmas and birthday his mother sends him a card, obviously as she is his mother, and that's what mums do. However, he cannot understand why she signs the cards thus: 'Lots of love, Mother (Jacqueline)'.

He's now worked out that the reason his mother writes her first name is because she doesn't want his wife to think that she is his wife's mother as well!

So the addition of her name is to clarify to his wife that the card is from his mother to him with her love, but that she is *not*

Shirley's mother.

This sort of behaviour can only come from someone who spends a lot of time thinking, and obviously over-thinking, as in this case!

Your Virgo mother wants to have everything in its place and a place for everything. She may not actually achieve this, but it will be her burning motivation.

And I would like to dispel a myth here. Not every Virgo is tidy. As in this example, physical things can be all over the place, but mentally their thoughts are very ordered.

Nicole is a mum, an author, astrologer and writer. She tells us about her ability for order.

'With physical "things" – not at all orderly; I can't even pretend it's organised chaos – it's just chaos. I'm very untidy and forever losing things, because I never bother to put them back where I got them from. There's a lot of clutter and mess in our home. I don't usually mind the clutter, but I do get annoyed with myself when items go missing. Periodically though (about once a week or ten days) the mess suddenly gets to me and becomes overwhelming, where a few hours earlier it didn't worry me at all – at that point I will spend a few hours manically tidying up, doing housework and organising my desk, but in between those times I'm afraid I don't really bother. In terms of mental organisation, however, it's a different story. I also love to make detailed written lists...which I then lose amid the household mess.'

Ah, the famous Virgo lists! Every Virgo, without exception, writes lists. If you know a Virgo who doesn't, please get in touch, but you'll find that they list things on their phones or Facebook pages or Twitter accounts, or they write and record detailed information.

So, physically with inanimate objects, Nicole isn't tidy, but when she describes her thought processes, we get the true Virgo picture of detail:

'I get very, very detailed when I plan or organise anything. In practical terms, that's a good thing, because I don't overlook the little details that make the whole thing work. On the other hand, I think I can be too detailed when it comes to trying to organise others. When my daughter was little, if she was worried about something like a school trip or a visit to the doctor, I would talk about it with her in great detail, explaining every step of the process: what would happen when, what she should do, what she could do if x happened, how she might feel if y happened. That did generally help her then, but now she's 13 and I still do the same thing, which exasperates her no end!'

Your Virgo mother will also be very in tune with health issues. Here's Scorpio Andrea talking about growing up with a Virgo mother:

'She had an unswervable faith in the National Health Service (born the same year that I was) and its practitioners, and treated the GP with the reverence others might reserve for the vicar. She reserved the same respect for the dentist and the health visitor. We were all taken to the clinic and the dental surgery to be weighed and examined at the right intervals…She could not stand contradiction, which, as a young child, made me nervous and I felt as if I was treading on egg shells. As I grew older and became more my own person, I would oppose her, often quite violently as I became strong-minded. She, in her way, was loving.'

If you remember the reason *why* your Virgo mother is so concerned about health issues – because being healthy is akin to respecting the body, the temple of the soul – you'll be less likely to disagree with her guidance.

Your Virgo Dad

You Virgo father is a rare and peculiar being. If you can get some insights into his behaviour, rather than just thinking 'Why did he do/say that?' you'll be in a better space.

Here's a young Gemini lady (with a Virgo Moon) who lives in northern Europe talking about her Virgo father:

'Having a Virgo dad is having everything in the house organised and in its place – books, vinyl records, tapes, everything. All in a particular order. And he'd always know if something had been moved even a millimetre…He was never angry about it or anything, but he just occasionally made us aware that he noticed those things.

'I never had a problem with it personally, but my mother (Taurus) said she feels like her freedom is being taken away because he notices. Also, a part of my love for linguistic accuracy is because of him. That deeply logical thinking of a true mathematician always showed in casual communication, friendly making fun of what I said if the words weren't of the exact meanings of what I meant to say or could be interpreted in a double meaning. While other people got annoyed – "Oh, you know what I meant!" – I found it fun most of the time. Now I think it was a great education – taught me to choose words carefully, so they would be as accurate as possible and to make that double meaning intentional, when I want to. Maybe it's my Virgo Moon, but all this striving for precision, accuracy and his perfectionism, which drove other people insane, was something I personally admired and enjoyed. He always encouraged me to ask fewer questions and to look things up and try to understand them myself. But when he did explain something, he managed to make the most complicated things sound simple as he could always find some sort of an analogy for an example, so I could picture things in my head and really "see the meaning". Because of him my favourite childhood book was an encyclopaedia, because there were always those lying around.

'There was never too much physical contact like hugs or kisses,

and he was rarely home, working a lot, but we bonded through learning, information, crossword solving, watching Discovery and National Geographic together, me sharing new interesting facts I'd read somewhere. And that was enough to know he loves me and cares. What I am trying to say is he was rarely home, but when he was, he shared an interest in the same things as I did and encouraged me to deepen the knowledge in those things. Through that, I've become closer to him than I ever was to my mother who was home a lot more. We still are close and have a very special relationship.'

Her account is not dissimilar to my Aquarius mother (who has Jupiter and Saturn in the fourth in Virgo) talking about her father (my grandfather) and how, when buying furniture for one of their houses, he 'was insistent that we each have our own desk'. This was so my mother and her two sisters could write letters and study.

To get on well with your Virgo dad, take some time to see further than all his idiosyncrasies and maybe even have a discussion with him if things aren't going how you'd like them to. Virgo dads are quite open to sensible discussion and you'll have a better result if you pose your questions in a gentle way without trying to make them seem wrong.

Your Virgo Sibling

As I have mentioned before, you're more likely to get along with someone if you're the same or complementary element as someone else.

Your Virgo sibling will be reasonably easy to get along with if you're a Water or Earth sign. The difficulties can start if you're an Air or Fire sign (taking into account things might be wonderful if you've got similar Moons or Ascendants).

You will need to remember to allow them space for hobbies and things they collect, but they won't be worried about fairness (leave that to the Libras) or who-gets-the-most-amount-of-attention (that's Leo territory) or freedom (that's for Sagittarius), but they will be particular about certain things. And once you find out what those 'certain things' are, you can make sure you avoid disturbing them, to ensure fluffy feelings all round.

If you're lucky, you'll get on with your Virgo sibling.

Here is a young Cancer lady talking about how her younger Virgo sister saved the day when their mom came back from hospital after brain surgery. As she's a Sun sign, Cancer, and her mother's primary caregiver (her mother also had ovarian cancer), she got all emotional about her mom being so ill, and instead of getting on and doing what was necessary, she says she went into 'shut-down':

> *'Anyway, my sister got here on Thursday and life got better for Mom and me. She encouraged me to (a) be nicer to myself, and (b) to get away from the house for the weekend. Which I totally did. Yay! A retreat! Then she laid some Virgo-love down – she cleaned and organized Mom's room, she cooked and cooked and stocked our refrigerator/freezer with homemade goodies, she ran errands, organized Mom's paperwork, and probably more stuff that I don't even know about. When I returned home on Sunday the atmosphere in the house was entirely different. And she made Easter lasagne, which was awesome.'*

This is a lovely example of how her Virgo sister helped out by doing what she is good at, which is organising things, and allowed her to recover her emotional equilibrium and be able to carry on with her caring role.

* * *

I hope you have enjoyed learning a little about the sign Virgo and a little about Astrology. If you would like some more information, do visit my website www.maryenglish.com.

I am writing this while the Moon is in Virgo, in the hot-spring city of Bath in the UK. I am a Pisces. I am happy in my job, with my son, with my lovely husband and with my family.

I know that all life is made from good and bad and I decided not so long ago to focus on the good. A candle is burning beside me and I am imagining the flame is burning to help you focus on the good too. If we all understood each other a little more, maybe we'd get on better.

I wish you all the happiness in the world...and peace too.

Mary

Astrological Chart Information and Birth Data

(from astro-databank at www.astro.com and www.astrotheme.com)

No accurate birth data

Michael Jackson, 29th August 1958, Gary IN, USA, Sun Virgo, Moon Pisces

Freddie Mercury, 5th September 1946, Zanzibar, Sun Virgo, Moon Sagittarius OR Scorpio

Roald Dahl, 13th September 1916, Cardiff, Wales, Sun Virgo, Moon Aries

H.G. Wells, 21st September 1866, Bromley, England, Moon Aquarius

Stephen Fry, 24th August 1957, Sun Virgo, Moon Leo

Stephen Russell (Barefoot doctor), 13th September 1954, London, 'before breakfast', Sun Virgo, Moon Pisces, poss Libra Asc

Lenny Henry, 29th August 1958, Dudley, England, Sun Virgo, Moon Pisces

John Peel, 30th August 1939, Liverpool, England, Sun Virgo, Moon Pisces

Billie Piper, 22nd September 1982, Swindon, Wiltshire, UK, Moon Scorpio

Leslie Hornby ('Twiggy'), 19th September 1949, London, unverified birth time, poss Cancer Ascendant, Sun in 2nd, Moon Leo

Leo Tolstoy, 9th September 1828, Cancer Ascendant, Tula, Russia, 10.52pm, Sun in 3rd, Moon Virgo (unverified)

Antonin Dvorak, 8th September 1841, Nelahozeves, Czech Republic, 11am (not verified), Sun Virgo, Moon Gemini

Ascendant

Gene Simmons, 25th August 1949, Haifa, Israel, 8.55pm, Aries

Ascendant, Sun in 5th, Moon in Virgo

Agatha Christie, 15th September 1890, Torquay, England, 4am, Virgo Ascendant, Sun in 1st, Moon Virgo

Chrissie Hynde, 7th September 1951, Akron OH, USA, 10am, Libra Ascendant, Sun in 11th, Moon Scorpio

Liz Greene, 4th September 1946, Englewood NJ, USA, 1.01pm, Scorpio Ascendant, Sun in 10th, Moon Sagittarius

D.H. Lawrence, 11th September 1885, Eastwood, England, 9.45am, Scorpio Ascendant, Sun in 11th, Moon Libra

Mother Teresa, 26th August 1910, Skopje, Macedonia, 2.25pm, Sagittarius Ascendant, Sun in 9th, Moon Taurus

Sophia Loren, 20th September 1934, Rome, Italy, 2.10pm, Capricorn Ascendant, Sun in 9th, Moon Aquarius

Larry Hagman, 21st September 1931, Fort Worth TX, USA, 4.20pm, Aquarius Ascendant, Sun in 8th, Moon in Aquarius

Peggy Lipton, 30th August 1946, New York NY, USA, 6.57pm, Aquarius Ascendant, Sun in 7th, Moon Libra

Jack Holliday, 27th August 1959, Whittier CA, USA, 7.53pm, Pisces Ascendant, Sun in 6th, Moon Gemini

Yao Ming, 12th September 1980, Shanghai, China, 7pm, Aries Ascendant, Sun in 6th, Moon Libra

Zipporah Dobyns, 26th August 1921, Chicago IL, USA, 9.48pm, Taurus Ascendant, Sun in 4th, Moon Gemini

Amy Winehouse, 14th September 1983, Enfield, England, 10.25pm, Gemini Ascendant, Sun in 4th, Moon Capricorn

Van Morrison, 31st August 1945, Belfast, N. Ireland, 11.59pm, Cancer Ascendant, Sun in 2nd, Moon Cancer

Maurice Chevalier, 12th September 1888, Paris, France, 2am, Leo Ascendant, Sun in 2nd, Moon Sagittarius

Leonard Cohen, 21st September 1934, Montreal, Canada, 6.45am, Pisces Ascendant, Sun in 12th, Moon Pisces

Peter Sellers, 8th September 1925, Southsea, England, 6am, Virgo Ascendant, Sun in 1st, Moon Taurus

Moon

Lauren Bacall, 16th September 1924, New York NY, USA, 2am, Cancer Ascendant, Sun in 2nd, Moon Aries

Marjorie Orr, 9th September 1944, Glasgow, Scotland, 10am, Libra Ascendant, Sun in 12th, Moon Gemini

Keanu Reeves, 2nd September 1964, Beirut, Lebanon, 5.41am, Virgo Ascendant, Sun in 12th, Moon Cancer

Queen Elizabeth I, 17th September 1533, Greenwich, England, 2.54pm, Capricorn Ascendant, Sun in 9th, Moon Taurus

Julie Kavner, 7th September 1950, Los Angeles CA, USA, 6.45pm, Pisces Ascendant, Sun in 7th, Moon Cancer

Edgar Dean Mitchell, 17th September 1930, 4.30am, Hereford TX, USA, Leo Ascendant, Sun in 1st, Moon Cancer

Buddy Holly, 7th September 1936, 3.30pm, Lubbock TX, USA, Capricorn Ascendant, Sun in 9th, Moon Gemini

Houses

Kenney Jones (drummer with The Who), 16th September 1948, London, England, 8.55pm, Taurus Ascendant, Moon Pisces, Sun in 5th

Edwin Moses, 31st August 1955, Dayton OH, USA, 7.58pm, Pisces Ascendant, Moon Aquarius, Sun in 6th

Pauline Collins, 3rd September 1940, Exmouth, England, 7.40pm, Pisces Ascendant, Moon Libra, Sun in 7th

Claudia Schiffer, 25th August 1970, Rheinberg, Germany, 12.10pm, Scorpio Ascendant, Moon Gemini, Sun in 10th

Further Information

The Astrological Association
www.astrologicalassociation.com
The Bach Centre, The Dr Edward Bach Centre, Mount
Vernon, Bakers Lane, Brightwell-cum-Sotwell, Oxon, OX10 0PZ,
UK www.bachcentre.com
Ethical Dating Site www.natural-friends.com

References

1. Christopher McIntosh, *The Astrologers and Their Creed: An Historical Outline*, Arrow Books, London, 1971
2. Christina Rose, *Astrological Counselling: A Basic Guide to Astrological Themes in Person to Person Relationships*, The Aquarian Press, Northamptonshire, 1982
3. Erin Sullivan, *Retrograde Planets: Traversing the Inner Landscape*, Arkana, Penguin Books, London, 1992
4. Northrop Frye, *The Secular Scripture*, Harvard University Press, 1976
5. H.G. Wells, *Experiment in Autobiography: Discoveries and Conclusions of a Very Ordinary Brain*, Victor Gollancz & The Cresset Press, 1934
6. http://digitaljournal.com/article/222107#ixzz1pefr2XiC
7. Colin Evans, *The New Waite's Compendium of Natal Astrology, with Ephemeris for 1880–1980 and Universal Table of Houses*, Routledge & Kegan Paul, London, 1967
8. Rae Orion, *Astrology for Dummies*, IDG Books Worldwide, Inc., Foster City, CA, 1999
9. Linda Goodman, *Love Signs: A New Approach to the Human Heart*, Pan Books, London, 1980
10. Laurence Hillman, *Planets in Play: How to Reimagine Your Life through the Language of Astrology*, Penguin Books, London, 2007
11. Marcia Starck, *Healing with Astrology*, The Crossing Press, California, 1998
12. https://groups.google.com/group/uk.railway/browse_thr ead/thread/6469752454660b2b/680b48d7b5824cd7%3Fq%3D %2522Geoffrey%2BHoyland%2522%23680b48d7b5824cd7&e i=iGwTS6eaOpW8Qpmqic0O&sa=t&ct=res&cd=2&source=gr oups&usg=AFQjCNEmymbwS9jQo1S16S1F-OZHeOs17A
13. D.H. Lawrence, *The Selected Letters of D.H. Lawrence*,

compiled by James T. Boulton, Press Syndicate, University of Cambridge, UK, 1997

14. http://www.veganmeans.com/vegan_who/Donald_Watson. htm

15. Maritha Pottenger, *Easy Astrology Guide: How to Read Your Horoscope*, ACS Publications, San Diego, California, 1991, 1996

Dodona Books offers a broad spectrum of divination systems to suit all, including Astrology, Tarot, Runes, Ogham, Palmistry, Dream Interpretation, Scrying, Dowsing, I Ching, Numerology, Angels and Faeries, Tasseomancy and Introspection.